FLYING PAST

Also by Mike Brooke

A Bucket of Sunshine: Life on a Cold War Canberra Squadron

Follow Me Through: The Ups and Downs of a RAF Flying Instructor

Trials and Errors: Experimental UK Test Flying in the 1970s

More Testing Times: Testing Flying in the 1980s and '90s

FLYING PAST

TALES OF DISPLAYING CLASSIC HISTORIC AIRCRAFT

MIKE BROOKE

In Memoriam

Pilots named in this book who died while flying historic aircraft:

Don Bullock

Neil Williams

Trevor Roche

Peter Treadaway

Euan English

Norman Lees

Mike Carlton

First published 2018

The History Press
The Mill, Brimscombe Port
Stroud, Gloucestershire, GL5 2QG
www.thehistorypress.co.uk

British Library Cataloguing in Publication Data.
A catalogue record for this book is available from the British Library.

ISBN 978 0 7509 8768 4

Typesetting and origination by The History Press
Printed and bound by CPI Group (UK) Ltd

Contents

Acknowledgements

To write one book and get it published is quite a challenge. To write five is bordering on sadomasochism! Although many hours, days and weeks are spent in seclusion at the keyboard, with only memories for company, it is not a solitary task. I am blessed by having wonderful people on whom I can rely; people who are selflessly generous with their time in helping to make the finished product so much better for you, the reader.

At the top of the long list of those willing helpers is my best friend and wife, Linda. For the past seven years she has supported me tirelessly through the adventure of reliving my flying life, in the medium of words and pictures. She has proofread hundreds of thousands of words, corrected grammar, spelling and punctuation, and often improved many of my phrases and ideas. She is, and has always been, the wind beneath my wings. Thank you, my darling.

They say that a picture is worth a thousand words; and whoever 'they' are, they are right! Hence, I must give a special vote of thanks to Peter March and Steven Jefferson, two really talented aviation photographers. They have looked through their extensive collections and have allowed me to use their work to enhance this volume. I'm sure that you will agree that their photographs are a superb contribution to the end product.

An important part of writing non-fiction is to ensure that the facts are true and not fiction. Although I have my flying logbooks, various notes, articles and other written work that I have kept over the years, my recollection of some of the detail may not have been totally accurate. Therefore, I am very grateful to fellow Shuttleworth Collection pilots, Dodge Bailey and George Ellis, for checking that section of the book for 'fake news'. I am also thankful that two books, given to me and signed by the author, the late David Ogilvy, provided valuable cross-checks on many elements. Also, I doff my hat to all those anonymous posters online who enable us twenty-first-century authors to discover things hitherto unknown; some of which actually prove useful!

Last, but by no means least, I am indebted to my publishers, The History Press, for offering me the opportunity, for the fifth time, to share my story. Especially I want to thank my editors, Amy Rigg and Alex Waite, who have continued to guide me and my book through the process of publication. I hope that you will agree that the final product is a credit to their colleagues at THP.

Mike Brooke
Ryde, Isle of Wight,
April 2018

Introduction

Aerobatics and Airshows

Although some of you will be familiar with many aerobatic manoeuvres, I thought I would start with a description of a selection of the airborne gyrations that you may come across in the course of reading the tales that follow. Those of you that are familiar with aerobatics, usually known to the cognisant as 'aeros', as well as the airshow scene, might want to skip to Chapter 1.

Aeros

The following is not intended as an instruction manual on aerobatics. If you want to know more there are many books on the topic, as well as lots of stuff online. However, it will be hard to improve on the descriptions and instruction given in the late, great Neil Williams' book *Aerobatics*, published by Airlife in 1975, with many reprints since. Neil was a test pilot and accomplished competitive aerobatic pilot, as well as being one of my predecessors at the Shuttleworth Collection. A measure of Neil's amazing skill and awareness was demonstrated when he landed safely after a structural wing failure in a Zlin aircraft. The failure meant that Neil had to fly inverted to hold the broken wing in place and then roll upright just before landing. The poor old Zlin was a write-off but Neil was unhurt. By this amazing bit of flying he proved the saying that any landing that you can walk away from is a good one!

There are two basic types of manoeuvres that take the aircraft and its pilot beyond the norms of up-and-away flying: that is turns, climbs and descents. These are manoeuvres with a vertical component and those with a horizontal flight path; then there's a third group with a combination of the two. A fundamental concept to grasp is that once aerobatics enter the flight envelope then the terms 'up' and 'down' can lose some of their meaning, especially as to where the nose of the aircraft is going in relation to the world outside and to the pilot. For instance, if I wish to fly upside down and maintain altitude then I have to push the nose 'down' in relation to myself, but 'up' in relation to the horizon I see out of the window. I will start by describing the purely vertical manoeuvres.

First, the **loop**. In the loop the aircraft is flown so as to describe a vertical circle in the sky; in fact the loop is usually not a perfect circle but a rounded ellipse. To do a successful loop sufficient initial speed and power is required for the aircraft to still be flying properly as it reaches the apex. If it doesn't then it may stall and fall back, and not achieve the desired flight path. At the appropriate entry conditions the pilot must pull the stick back to achieve an acceleration towards the vertical. The G-force will vary with aircraft type and entry speed, but it should be sufficient to get the aircraft safely onto its back at the top of the loop. This G-force will reduce as the speed falls and then increase again on the way down. The aim should be to finish the loop at the same height and speed as the entry. To ensure that the loop is actually vertical the wings must be kept parallel to the horizon using lateral stick inputs and, especially on prop-driven aircraft, the slip ball must be monitored and kept central using the rudder pedals. A successful loop requires practice and application; if you have got it right you might well be rewarded by the satisfying bump of flying through your own slipstream as you approach the completion of the loop.

Next the **stall turn**: not all types of aircraft can perform this safely. The manoeuvre starts like a loop but once the aeroplane is in the vertical attitude, on the way up the pilot must stop the nose from pitching over any further and hold it there. That's done by reference to the horizon viewed to the left and right; experience will play a part in knowing when the aircraft is travelling truly vertically. Then the pilot uses the stick to keep things steady. After a period of time, which will depend on the power-to-weight ratio of the aircraft, the speed will fall towards zero. At the latest possible stage, again learned by experience, full rudder is applied in the chosen direction. This will cause a rotation about the centre of the fuselage (yaw) and this must be continued until the aircraft is pointing vertically down. Aileron control may have to be used during this rotation to prevent the wings rolling out of the vertical. After stopping the yaw with rudder the pilot then holds the vertical descent until the right moment to pull the stick back and regain the height at which the manoeuvre was started. In prop-driven aeroplanes the slipstream from the propeller over the rudder will help the aircraft around the 'turn' at lower speeds than in jets. The stall turn is not usually performed in swept-wing, jet aircraft because of their strong dihedral effect, which makes the aircraft roll strongly when it is yawed. There is also much more chance of a spin developing if things go awry. There are variations that can be flown using the stall turn, such as the hesitation variant, where the yaw is carried out in four stages, using opposite rudder to achieve the hesitations in the yaw rate. Then there is the 'noddy' stall turn where the aircraft is fish-tailed on the way up into the manoeuvre. More advanced versions include the Lomcovák, named after its Czech inventor, where a spin is initiated at the top and stopped when the nose is below the horizon again. There are even more adaptations involving negative rapid rolls and more prolonged descending rotations but those need not concern us mere mortals and are the preserve of that special breed of aerobatic aviators.

Moving on to the horizontal or rolling aerobatics: the first and easiest is the **aileron roll**. This is what it says on the tin: a 360-degree (or more) roll carried out using only the ailerons through the application of (usually) full lateral stick. Because the nose normally drops a little during the roll it is good practice to raise the nose above the horizon as viewed from the cockpit before the roll is started. High-performance jets can achieve eye-watering roll rates; for instance, the Folland Gnat trainer would roll at 420 degrees per second with full aileron applied at around 350kt. The lower the performance the lower the roll rate and the more the nose will drop. Much more eye-pleasing, but also much more difficult, is the **slow roll**. The aim of this is to fly a horizontal flight path while rolling the aircraft through 360 degrees at a rate of about 20–30 degrees per second, so taking around twelve to eighteen seconds to complete the roll. These figures are only a suggestion and are a good start point for training. The control inputs to complete a smooth, level slow roll without changing heading are complex to describe without using one's hands and require repeated practice to learn. Suffice it to say here that all three control surfaces (elevator, aileron and rudder) need to be used to achieve the desired result. A slow roll will often end with the controls being crossed. However, once the technique is mastered then it will transfer to all aircraft types; it will just be the magnitude of the ever-changing inputs around the roll that may alter. By combining some of these control inputs at set points around a rapid aileron roll then **four-point** and **eight-point**

hesitation rolls can be performed. In high-performance aeroplanes these can be impressive to watch.

Now the trainee aerobatic pilot can learn to blend rolls and loops to create even more manoeuvres. The first of these is the **barrel roll**. This manoeuvre, like the slow roll, is best experienced than described. However, it is essentially a loop carried out while rolling slowly. But, because of the roll, unlike the loop, it does not turn back on itself but progresses forward, while describing a graceful climb and descent. The name of the barrel roll helps one visualise its shape: imagine the aeroplane being flown round the inside of an old-fashioned wooden barrel. To fly it successfully requires just the right combination of pull, like a loop, and roll, like an aileron roll.

Another combination of the loop and roll is the **roll-off-the-top**. This manoeuvre is sometimes known as the Immelmann turn, named after its supposed inventor German First World War fighter pilot, Max Immelmann (21 September 1890–18 June 1916). He was credited with being the first pilot to achieve a kill using a synchronised machine gun and was the first German airman to be awarded the prestigious gallantry medal *Pour le Mérite*, also known as the Blue Max. To carry out this manoeuvre the first half of a loop is flown and then when the aircraft is inverted at the apex, the second half of a slow roll is flown so that the aircraft ends up flying in the opposite direction, level and at a higher altitude. Success depends on having sufficient energy at the top to carry out the roll safely. For those of a steelier outlook and flying aircraft with a good power to weight ratio, the roll-off-the-top can, if sufficient speed remains, be converted to a **vertical eight**. This is done by simply flying a second full loop all the way round to the horizontal and then making the first half of a slow roll followed by a half loop down to the original entry altitude. Speed control is an issue in this latter part of the manoeuvre and high G-levels may ensue. The finished product should look like its name: a figure eight vertically in the sky.

The figure eight can also be flown so that it lies on its side in the sky; this is known as the **Cuban** or **horizontal eight**. This manoeuvre starts from a looping entry but the loop is stopped after the apex is passed, with the aircraft inverted and the nose 30–45 degrees below the horizon. The wings are then rolled through 180 degrees and the dive continued to the initial entry height, when the manoeuvre is repeated – that will then achieve the figure eight with the aircraft back where it started. Half of this manoeuvre can be flown and is especially useful during air displays for turning around at the end of the display line – it is known as the **half Cuban 8**.

If this figure is reversed, that is the aircraft is rolled on the way up and then the loop is completed from there, it is known as – guess what – the **half reverse Cuban 8**.

Airshows

There are many hundreds of airshows held annually around the world. These vary from huge international events (such as the trade shows held at Le Bourget near Paris, Farnborough near London, and in Dubai or Singapore), to the fly-in events on countless grass airfields in many nations. In 2015 there were 245 notified civil and military air displays in the UK. Again these varied in size and content from the Royal International Air Tattoo, with its eight-hour flying display, to the small, more intimate affairs held at flying club level. The usual UK statistic quoted by many in the business (and a big business it is too) is that annual attendance at airshows is second only to that at football matches.

The regulation of airshows has developed over the more than 100 years since those magnificent men first showed off their flying machines to an eager and inquisitive public. Initially the thrill consisted solely of seeing the fragile stick and string constructions simply take to the air and land safely again; one did not automatically lead to the other. That was probably another magnetic draw for the Edwardian crowds. However, very few aviators actually died in exhibiting their bravado and skill (or lack of it!).

The rules governing the application for an aerial event, its conduct and supervision have built themselves into voluminous tomes. These are usually written and amended by the national aviation regulatory authority; in the UK the Civil Aviation Authority (CAA); in the USA the Federal Aviation Administration (FAA); and so on. In parallel with these regulations, many country's military authorities issue rules for airshows held at military locations, or for the participation of military aircraft in other public aerial events. Nowadays, the civil and military rules are usually well-harmonised. The aim of the whole shebang is to ensure that the aviation authority's very basic remit is met; that is that nothing shall fall from the sky and hit anyone or do damage to property.

The supervision of each show is given to a nominated person, often known as the display director, and he or she will ensure that the rules are followed to the letter. Often a flying control committee (FCC) will be formed to help supervise and approve all the participants' routines. FCC members are usually seasoned pilots with flying display experience. The display pilot has to know all the regulations pertaining to exactly where he can fly during his display and to what minimum heights and maximum speed he must adhere.

He will be required to submit his routine for prior approval and fly it for the FCC to view and, if appropriate, comment on before the airshow happens. All UK and US display pilots will have been observed by an approved experienced airshow pilot beforehand and given a display authorisation, which will denote any limitations on the pilot's minimum altitude and whether or not he may fly in formation during a display. Another rule that is, these days, rigidly applied, certainly in the UK, is that non-operating crew cannot be flown in the aircraft during a public display; so no giving your best pal a seat during your show.

The onus for self-discipline, knowledge, experience and practice on display pilots is heavy. The pilot who wants to fly in an airshow has to know not only his aircraft's handling, performance and limitations intimately, but also know his own limitations and stick to them in equal measure. Apart from peer pressure, there may be commercial or kudos factors that may drive pilots to try too hard. There's also the weather, especially cloud and wind that can disrupt the practised pattern of the display. Another factor that crops up from time to time is just that – timing. Generally speaking, airshow timings slip to the right and often organisers will try to get back on schedule with short-notice requests to pilots to cut a bit out of their routine. I've also experienced the opposite when an item has dropped out and one is both urged to get airborne sooner and fly a 'longer slot'. It's easy to sit in isolation and say that you won't do these things but with thousands of the paying public watching you feel a strong urge to help out. That's when it can get dangerous!

Another thing to be aware of is that each event will have a ground plan that lays out the very important display line. This is usually a feature that is easily seen from above and must not be crossed so that the hurtling machinery is kept at the regulation safe distance from the crowd line. Other features on and around the venue may be marked for no over-flight below a certain height. Finally, the pilots will be given all the radio frequencies that they should use both before and during the airshow and any airspace restrictions that may affect them within the local area.

There have been hundreds of lives lost at public air displays over the past century or more, and each one of those has led to a tightening of the rules. The control and oversight of all those involved in airshows has become intense in recent years and I know that things have changed greatly in the almost twenty years since I last flew a public display flight. So some of what appears in my tales would no longer be allowed – but it was then!

The best pre-show final brief I know goes as follows:

'Thrill the ignorant – impress the professionals – frighten no one.'

Part 1

THE BEGINNINGS

1

Aerobatic Training

VAMPIRE T11

I entered RAF flying training in May 1962; I was two weeks beyond my eighteenth birthday. I had already been a pilot for two years, but only of gliders and sailplanes. Now I was about to embark on a one-year course, during which I would fly more than 160 hours in the RAF's first jet-powered basic trainer, the Hunting Percival Jet Provost; known variously as the 'JP' or the 'Constant Thrust, Variable Noise Machine'! During that training course aerobatics would feature prominently alongside other required skills, such as night, instrument and formation flying (not, of course, at the same time!) and low- and high-level navigation. One of the offshoots of aerobatic instruction was learning the art of stringing several manoeuvres together and then, towards the end of the course, designing a sequence that could be flown in relation to a fixed point on the ground: the essentials of an air display. Those of us who showed enough aptitude at that part of the syllabus would participate in the end-of-course aerobatic competition.

Although this event would not be flown at low-level over the airfield, our efforts would be judged by an accompanying flying instructor, at a safe altitude over a prominent ground feature – often a disused airfield, with which early 1960s Britain was liberally littered.

Thinking caps were dusted off and we students were encouraged to bring together our aerobatic repertoires into a cohesive and flowing sequence, during which we had to adhere to a minimum altitude and maintain our position in relation to the nominated ground feature. Those of us who had been told that we would be taking part in the competition for the aerobatic prize would be allowed a couple of extra flying hours to practice, but no more.

Cometh the day, cometh the man. And that man was the figure of an instructor from another flight or one with whom one had never flown. The briefing would be concise and cover the mandatory minimum or base altitude, usually 5,000ft, and the location for the eight- to ten-minute sequence of manoeuvres. The student would furnish the instructor with a copy of his display sequence and the instructor would ensure that the student understood who was in charge.

'Enjoy yourself, but don't frighten me,' was the nearest thing to encouragement that one could expect from the man in the other seat. He would spend the majority of the short sortie that followed in taciturn silence. Well, one hoped that he would! On landing, not much would be said as he had to confer with the other supervising instructors about which student pilot they thought most worthy of the prize. If not flown over the home base then the competition was judged solely from the air. I was fortunate enough to compete in such competitions at both basic and advanced training levels, as well as at the end of my instructor's course. I never won – but came second, twice!

One initially challenging, but ultimately somewhat amusing, incident occurred during a practice session for the aerobatic competition at the end of my advanced flying training course. It was 1963 and we were flying the venerable de Havilland Vampire, one of the first British jet aircraft. The Vampire had been designed in the early 1940s and first flew in 1943. The version we flew at our flying training school was the two-seat trainer, known as the Vampire T.11, which had side-by-side ejection seats crammed into its rather small cockpit.

On the day in question, I had gone off on my own to fly my display routine and had made my way to a disused wartime airfield only five minutes' flying time from our base at RAF Swinderby, near Newark. I set up for the first manoeuvre, which was an arrival at 420kt and the base altitude of 5,000ft at 90 degrees to my chosen display line, which was the main runway. I then pulled 5g into a vertical climb, during which my aim was to roll through 270 degrees and then carry out a loop along the display line. However, as the G came on there was a bit of a bang and I found my view out of the window disappeared. The seat pan had collapsed beneath me and the top of the Vampire's rather long stick was now right in front of my face! I was still hurtling skyward and had no real idea which way was up! I decided to push the stick forward and keep full power on the engine until I could see what was going on. As the aircraft followed a nose-down trajectory I became weightless and I floated up in the cockpit with the seat still firmly attached to my bottom by its straps. Once I had found the horizon, I levelled off – and immediately disappeared back into the bowels of the cockpit!

I reached down to find the large lever that raised and lowered the seat – all the while flying as straight and level as I could by reference to the instruments, because I couldn't see anything useful out of the window! I found the lever and tried to depress the plunger that released the locking mechanism, which normally allowed the pilot to set the seat pan at the right height. It wasn't there! The lever could no longer be moved. The whole thing had jammed at its lowest position. As I was a pilot with a very short back length I usually had the seat set at its highest position; now I was stuck with an extremely limited view of the outside world, flying along at about 300kt.

Befitting its vintage and initial role as a fighter, the Vampire did not possess an autopilot or significant navigation aids. However, I knew that I wasn't that far from base so I put out a radio call explaining my predicament and requesting a heading to steer to come home. Once I had received that crucial bit of information I turned the jet onto the required heading and flew along using the instruments, all the while wondering how I was going to land without being able to see the ground.

It wasn't long before the air traffic controller told me to reduce altitude and call the local controller before joining the visual circuit. I did so.

'Roger, Delta 36, report when you have the airfield in sight,' he said. He obviously hadn't thought things through.

I rolled the aircraft nearly inverted briefly and looked up to see if I could spot any recognisable local ground features. Sure enough, I spotted the edge of the airfield and turned left to carry out an orbit until I had worked out what to do.

'Delta 36 is holding overhead at 1,500ft,' I announced. 'I can't see out very well so I'm going to loosen my straps and see if I can get a bit higher in the cockpit.'

This initiated a response from the duty instructor. 'Delta 36, put your ejection seat safety pins back in and then unstrap and try to move across into the other seat,' he said. Either he was a tiny person or he'd forgotten just how little room there was in here! In these situations it was best not to argue, but rather give the impression that you would comply.

'Roger,' I said.

In the event I could not reach the holes at the top of the seat for one of the safety pins but I did replace the one at the bottom, between my legs. I then loosened off the straps and pushed upwards with my feet on the floor, this resulted in a bit of undulating flight while I locked myself in a semi-upright position. But now I could see out well enough to land.

'Delta 36 is downwind to land,' I announced, as confidently as I could muster.

'Roger, 36, you are number one,' came the reply.

I flew the well-practised pattern until I was pointing at the runway, flaps and wheels down and with a clearance to land. As I passed 300ft, at just the right speed, I was congratulating myself in overcoming the problem. Then it struck me that after landing I would need to use my set of presently out-of-reach rudder pedals to keep straight, or at least avoid swerving off the runway, while applying the brakes with the lever on the stick. So the last thirty seconds of concentration on a decent arrival were disturbed with working out what to do once I was down.

After the bump announcing contact with *terra firma* I let myself fall back into a sitting position with my feet going forward onto the rudder pedals and I started braking. As I could no longer see the runway in front of me I used the compass heading as a guide and craned upward to look over the side of the cockpit canopy, which was a bit lower than the windscreen ahead. That way I could see the edge of the runway and avoid any tendency to take a cross-country shortcut back to the dispersal area. It worked and I came to a walking pace about two-thirds of the way down the runway. The taxiway turn was, fortuitously, on my left so I kept going until I was clear of the runway, came to a stop, raised the flaps and got back on the radio.

'Delta 36 – is clear and shutting down – please send a tractor to tow me in.'

But the funny things that happened to me weren't over. The technical fault that caused the seat pan failure was just that. However, I returned to base with a self-inflicted fault on my next sortie.

This time I had got all the way through my aerobatic sequence success-fully, three times, and was about to come home. But I had earlier watched one of our instructors practising his air display routine, which had finished with him flying inverted and extending the undercarriage prior to making an inverted turn onto final approach to land; he rolled upright once lined up with the runway. It looked good so I thought I'd try it before I went home; I wouldn't get another chance.

Having rolled inverted and pushed on the stick to fly level, I checked that the speed was below the limit of 190kt and lowered the landing gear. That seemed to go well enough so I started an inverted left-hand turn. Of course, at 5,000ft I had nothing to line up with so I straightened up and, still flying upside down, I reached down to raise the undercarriage. I grasped the appropriate lever with my left hand and pulled. It wouldn't budge. I tried a bit harder – still unmovable. *Hey ho,* I thought, *leave it down and go home a bit slower than usual.*

When I arrived at the 'line hut', where we signed the aircraft back over to the techies, I wrote the following in the aircraft's RAF Form 700, its technical log: 'While inverted I selected the undercarriage down (up) and after 30 seconds I tried to select it up (down) and the lever would not move. Returned with the u/c locked down.'

Some time later I was ordered back to the line hut for words with the SNCO in charge. I walked in and a small crowd of chaps was gathered with the redoubtable 'Chiefy', who was fixing me with a steely glare. I could tell that I was not at the top of his popularity list.

'Ah, Mr Brooke. We took your kite into the hangar, jacked it up and plugged in the hydraulic rig and guess what, sir?' (The latter syllable came with that degree of cutting cynicism that SNCOs reserve for very junior officers in the wrong!)

'It worked?' I ventured.

'Yes – several times. Fault not found. Now then, do you know what stops anyone from retracting the undercarriage when the aircraft's on the ground?' The 'young fellah, me lad' was left unsaid.

'Yes, chief; it's the on-weight micro-switches,' I replied, with a smile to abate his underlying impatience.

'And what makes them work?'

'The weight of the aeroplane squashes the undercarriage legs and closes the micro-switches,' I replied, with a confident air.

'And what is it that they activate to stop you raising the undercart?' This was getting like the technical ground school exam all over again. And this time I either didn't know or couldn't remember. The result was the same.

'I don't know chief.'

'Well, young sir, there's a steel rod that slides across to stop you being able to raise the undercarriage lever. Simple, innit?' The 'just like you' also remained unsaid.

'So there you are, for reasons that I can't fathom, you're flying upside down and you push the undercart lever down. It works and the wheels go out into the fresh air. As you fly along, still upside down, the wheels, which weigh quite a bit, get pulled towards the aeroplane by gravity and close the micro-switches. So the rod slides into place and when you go to pull the lever to get the undercarriage back inside the aeroplane, it won't budge. It's doing exactly what it's supposed to do because nobody ever thought that one day some little pilot officer would come along and do what you did. If you'd have put the kite the right way up and then retracted the undercarriage it would have worked as advertised and it would 'ave saved my boys from a couple of hours' work.'

'I see,' I rejoined meekly. 'Sorry.' The 'I won't do it again' remained unsaid.

I didn't win the aerobatic trophy. Part of the reason was that I flew with a very large Canadian Air Force instructor, with us on an exchange posting. His arms and legs kept getting in the way of some of the more extreme movements I had to make with the control stick – that's my excuse and I'm sticking to it!

Within a few weeks I moved on to learn to fly the Canberra bomber and I thought that my aerobatic display days were over; I was wrong! However, through the RAF's excellent flying training system I had learnt many skills that would stay with me throughout the next forty years. Aerobatics and formation flying were just two that I would use in many future arenas.

2

Canberra Displays

CANBERRA B(1)8

Those of you who have read my first book, *A Bucket of Sunshine*, may recall that, in 1966, my navigator Geoff Trott and I were selected as the RAF Germany Canberra display crew. We were then in the middle of a three-year tour of duty with No. 16 Squadron, based at RAF Laarbruch in West Germany. We were flying the B(I)8 version of the English Electric Canberra jet bomber and the squadron had two roles. The primary one was the low-level, day and night delivery of tactical nuclear weapons on targets in Eastern Europe. The bomb (the eponymous 'Bucket of Sunshine') was carried in a bay underneath the aircraft that had hydraulically operated doors. We were part of NATO's potential response to any incursion across the Inner German Border (IGB) by Warsaw Pact or nuclear forces. In effect, that made us also part of the international nuclear deterrent. Our other role, which was not a NATO role but a national one, was that of conventional, low-level ground-attack; again we had to be proficient by day and night. For this mission the aircraft was fitted with four 20mm cannon in a gun pack, fitted in the bomb bay, and could also carry up to six 1,000lb HE bombs, as well as flares for night attack. Unlike in the nuclear role, for this work we usually flew around in formations of two or four and, very occasionally, eight aircraft.

The twin-jet Canberra was first designed in the 1940s to fulfil the role of a high-altitude, high-speed (for its day) bomber. It could fly as high as 50,000ft. It was developed during the 1950s through several versions, ending with the PR.9 photographic reconnaissance version that saw service into the 1990s. The B(I)8 version was the same size as the original bomber, with a fuselage length of 69ft and a similar wingspan. The engines had a thrust of 7,500lb and the aircraft could weigh up to 50,000lb with a full load of weapons and fuel. The Canberra's conventional flying controls were manually operated, no hydraulic assistance was provided, and its maximum allowed airspeed was 450kt.

On the squadron we flew mostly at very low altitudes, normally at 250ft above the ground by day or 600ft at night. If we had to go any great distance, like flying to the Mediterranean air bases that the RAF operated in those days, we normally transited at between 40,000 and 45,000ft and cruised at 0.74 Mach (74 per cent of the speed of sound). The Canberra was a simple and rugged aeroplane that could be demanding and tiring to fly during high-speed manoeuvring. It was especially difficult if an engine failed, especially at low airspeeds. Many aircrew had been killed following engine failures and we practised this emergency, especially on the T.4 trainer version; at Laarbruch we had access to two of these.

For an aircraft that was about as long as a Lancaster bomber and weighed around 20 tonnes, the Canberra was surprisingly agile. We did not practise aerobatics as such, but our initial nuclear delivery mode, with the acronym LABS (from the installed Low Altitude Bombing System) finished with a roll-off-the-top manoeuvre. This was started from 250ft and 430kt with a 3.4g pull-up in the vertical. At a pre-calculated angle (usually about 65 degrees) the bomb would be automatically released and fly a parabolic path towards the target, reaching a height of about 10,000ft before descending. It was equipped with a small radar altimeter that would make the bomb explode at about 1,500ft above the target; this made our bomb an 'air-burst' nuclear weapon.

During our ground-attack gun and bomb attack patterns we often flew wingover manoeuvres, during which bank angles beyond the vertical were achieved. These also gave us the opportunity to explore the relationships between speed and available turning performance and discover where the boundaries of the stall were.

When my squadron commander, aka 'The Boss', Wing Commander 'Trog' Bennett, called me into his office one day in spring 1966 I was quite taken aback at what he proposed.

'Noddy (my nickname at the time), I want you to design a flying display routine of about ten minutes duration.'

'Really, sir?' I responded excitedly. 'Who's going to fly it?' I really wasn't expecting a Junior Joe like me to be let loose in front of the public.

'You are, you chump. If I approve it I'll send it up the line to the station commander and he'll pass it up to HQ. Get cracking!' So off I went to put some pretty lines on paper and think deeply about how best to show off our bomber to the public.

I drew on my RAF training and considered the aircraft's limitations and how I could blend the variations of speed and manoeuvre into something flowing, and perhaps a little bit impressive or even exciting. I decided that I would submit two sequences: one for an overhead arrival at the airshow venue and another that commenced from take-off and went straight into a display. The latter would be more difficult, as I would be starting with no initial energy, whereas arriving at 450kt would not only be an impressive entrance, but give me lots of options. The arrival routine would be from the rear of the crowd at whatever minimum height I would be permitted. In those days arriving from behind the crowd was not only allowed, but was a popular option. Today it is totally *verboten*!

The two sequences were written down, sent up the line and came back in due course with an approval to start practices. This meant that I would practise the arrival option first, starting at a minimum altitude of 3,000ft above ground level over the airfield. In fact, I practised single elements of the routine before that, away from the airfield in free airspace and away from built-up areas. When I was confident that I could start stringing the elements together, and think about positioning, I received authorisation to practise overhead Laarbruch, usually late in the day. As my confidence and ability increased I started to reduce the minimum heights. The aim was to fly the sequence well enough to present it to the Boss and the station commander so that they could recommend to the Commander-in-Chief RAF Germany that I was fit to be let loose on the great European public.

Our display sequence started from behind the crowd rear at a speed of 450kt. As I passed over the crowd, I throttled the engines back and opened the bomb doors; the ensuing large 'hole' under the fuselage resulted in a booming noise, a very large version of blowing across the top of an empty bottle. It was a great attention getter. After crossing the display line, now doing about 330kt, I started a hard turn to the left and kept the bomb doors open. When we came round to abeam the crowd on the display line, hopefully at crowd centre, they would see the underside of the Canberra at a bank angle of about 60 degrees; the big wing would look quite impressive. I continued the turn, reducing speed, closed the bomb doors and, when the speed was below 190kt, lowered the landing gear. I needed more power to hold the speed at about 150kt so that I could lower the flaps. Now my flying technique had to be delicate as the steep bank angle could induce a stall if I let the speed drop any further. I also had to think about an engine failure and have enough control in hand to recover; especially should the engine on the lower wing fail. A way of doing that was to allow the aircraft to climb a bit on the far side of the turn; this would not be that obvious to the crowd as the perspective from their viewpoint would mask it.

At the completion of this final, quite tight turn I would raise the flaps and undercarriage as I rolled out, aiming about 30 degrees off the display line away from the crowd, holding the jet level, applying full power, accelerating and then climbing steeply to a point just beyond the end of the display line. The aim was to gain height to about 1,500ft and perform a steep wingover back onto the display line, descending back to my minimum height of 200ft and accelerating to be at about 350kt at crowd centre. In my original plan this would have been the initiation point for a steep upward roll, but this had been taken out of the routine by the worthies at HQ RAF Germany. So my modified routine was to initiate an offset loop, which is a steep turn flown at an angle of about 60 degrees to the horizontal. The height at the far side was about 3,000ft – but I could adjust that for cloud if necessary.

Accelerating back to crowd centre gave me lots of energy for a low pass along the display line, achieving a speed of around 400kt by the end of the crowd line. A hard 45-degree turn away and pull-up into a wingover using about 120 degrees of bank and retaining full power allowed me to roll out on the display line and, at 200ft, accelerate to 430–50kt and pull up into a LABS manoeuvre (roll-off-the-top) to finish the display. That usually meant that I was at 5,500ft above the airfield at the end. If I was not landing at the venue then I would depart from there, otherwise I would position for landing while the next event was taking place.

If I was already at the display venue and flying straight into the display, then the routine had to be modified. The advantage gained here was that I could use the minimum amount of fuel, so improving the power to weight ratio and hence performance. However, for structural reasons I had to carry 3,000lb in each integral wing tank and a mandatory minimum of 1,500lb in the centre fuselage tank. To be safe I would carry about 1,000lb in the front and rear tanks, so giving a total fuel weight of 9,500lb, as against a usual total internal fuel load of 16,000lb. The extra performance meant that the take-off ground roll could be as little as 1,500ft, so my navigator would calculate the take-off distance and then I would taxi forward on the runway so that lift-off would occur at crowd centre. By holding the nosewheel down to about 140kt I could then make a more rapid than normal rotation, simultaneously raising the undercarriage and holding 160kt in a steep climb. At 500ft I would turn away from the crowd and then reverse the turn and descend to 200ft and return along the display line to crowd centre. Once there and flying at about 350kt I could enter a steep, 3.5g turn and follow the arrival display sequence from there.

It turned out that our squadron had also been tasked with providing a formation display at the Hanover Airshow in early May 1966. The Boss had accepted the challenge and he'd delegated the design of that display to the A Flight commander. My solo slot was to be incorporated into the Hanover display and then I would be allocated individual airshow slots through the summer.

During the various displays that we gave during 1966 a couple of interesting incidents occurred. The first was during the six-aircraft formation that we had worked up for the aforementioned Hanover International Airshow. On approaching Hanover Airport I was in the close line-astern position on the Boss, with the other four in two echelon pairs each side of him. My nav, Geoff, was lying down in the nose ready to do his bit by calling out speeds and heights during our solo display.

Being the good navigator that he was, Geoff was following our progress towards the large international airport. At about two minutes to our overhead arrival he said, 'He's lined up on the wrong runway!'

'Are you sure?' I said.

'Yes! The airshow is happening on the south side and he's lined up with the northern runway!'

'OK, I'll tell him,' I said.

Just as I was about to press the transmit button, the Boss's voice came over the ether. 'Hang on men! Turning right – GO!'

Of course, I had the easy slot, but the guys on each side had to work very hard to stay in position as we wheeled this big formation onto the correct heading. As soon as we had rolled out I had to peel off into the first part of my sequence, the steep turns, while the rest of the guys continued east, turned around and changed formation. When they returned over the airfield and flew past, I rolled out and flew under them, exiting stage left. When they had passed I went back in accelerating to 400kt plus so that I could once more fly under the returning formation and fly the LABS manoeuvre. I waited and watched from 5,000ft until they had finished and were heading west again. I then went down to rejoin them for the flight back to Laarbruch. The final fillip to a great day was the pre-briefed arrival at base via individual LABS manoeuvres. We flew in from the east in loose line astern at 250ft and 430kt and as we each came abeam the control tower we pulled up into our half loops. We then had to make rapid descents, slowing down to landing speed and try to land in the same order that we had arrived in. I must admit that I'd had grave doubts about this, thinking that it would look a bit of a shambles. But it worked and the squadron mates gave us a round of applause as we taxied back in!

Another noteworthy incident happened when we were tasked to do a display at an airfield quite close to the Czech border. Because we had to fly so close to 'enemy territory' special procedures had to be applied. One of these included advice from the intelligence community not to follow any radio instructions to head east if they did not appear valid. I must admit that I thought that was a bit melodramatic. But when we had established radio and visual contact with our display venue, I heard a second voice saying, 'Canberra, head 090 degrees (*i.e. east*)'; this instruction was repeated several times. As we were now north of the airfield heading south, I knew that this was spurious – I ignored these repeated calls and just got on with the display routine. When we departed I changed frequency back to the military radar unit and reported the event. The controller implied that it was not at all unusual; the intelligence guys were right after all!

I very much enjoyed displaying the Canberra and felt truly privileged to have been selected to do it. It was a great introduction to the discipline and left me with the desire to do more – but just when that might arise again was very much an unknown.

3

The Red Devils

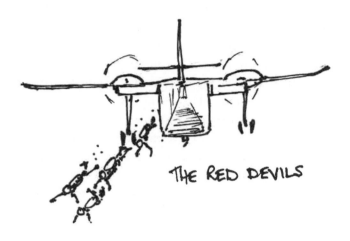

THE RED DEVILS

Twelve years later, in 1978, I was an experimental test pilot at the Royal Aircraft Establishment (RAE) Farnborough in Hampshire. In that job I was flying a wide variety of mainly well-established, sometimes old, aircraft, such as the Buccaneer, Hunter, Canberra, Varsity and Devon. I would often find myself flying three of these types on any one day. Doing this soon teaches you to reduce everything to its basics and recognise the common features of widely differing aircraft types: fundamental things, such as the throttles go forward to increase thrust and when you pull the stick back the houses get smaller. Instrument panel layouts vary a lot, but the basic six instruments can usually be found somewhere near the middle. Those six are the artificial horizon, compass, vertical speed indicator, turn and slip indicator, airspeed indicator and altimeter. With these six a pilot should be able to fly his aircraft effectively and safely even without reference to the outside world.

The joy of flying a variety of types of aircraft just makes you want even more diversity. So when another Farnborough-based pilot approached me with just such an offer, I couldn't refuse. He was Dave Peet, who was with the Meteorological Research Flight.

'How would you like to fly the Britten-Norman Islander for the Red Devils parachute display team? It'll involve flying at the weekends,' he said, perhaps expecting me to turn the offer down. Dave was already doing some of their flying and had been asked if he could find another pilot to take up some of the slack.

'Oh, that'll be fine with me, Dave, but I'll check with "management" at home,' I replied. I did and no objections were raised, so I told Dave that I was looking forward to learning how to drop people instead of bombs! Dave lent me a copy of the operating manual for the BN-2A Islander and said that he'd arrange a check flight with the team's senior pilot.

The Red Devils Parachute Display Team had originally formed in 1964, initially known as the Parachute Regiment Display Team: the 'Red Devils' sobriquet came later. Their first aircraft was a DH Dragon Rapide, a 1930s twin-engined biplane. But in the 1970s they were given the use of a dedicated BN-2A Islander, painted all red and registered G-AXDH. It was a nice touch in that DH (Delta Hotel) is the code used for a 'direct hit' in the delivery of airborne air-to-ground weapons; it was now being applied to bodies!

The Britten-Norman BN-2A Islander is a 1960s British designed, light utility passenger and cargo aircraft. It first flew in May 1965. Although designed more than fifty years ago, several hundreds are still in service with military and commercial operators around the world. Early models of the Islander were manufactured at Britten-Norman's factory on the Isle of Wight. Later variants were built in Romania, and then shipped to the Avions Fairey production facility in Belgium for finishing, before being flown to the UK for flight certification.

The Islander is a rugged but light, all-metal aeroplane with relatively long 45ft-span wings that have a high-lift cross section, so giving good load-carrying and short take-off and landing capabilities. The wings are mounted on top of the square-section, 39ft-long fuselage that can seat up to nine passengers. Entry to the cabin is by two wide doors, one on each side of the fuselage. The two-place pilots' cockpit is accessed by another door on the left side; the aircraft can be operated safely by a single pilot. The tricycle undercarriage is fixed down and there are electrically operated flaps. Foot-operated brakes and nosewheel steering, operated by the rudder pedals, help with manoeuvring and braking on the ground. The BN-2A version is fitted with two Lycoming O-540-E engines, each of which gives 260hp at maximum output, via variable pitch, feathering propellers. In 1978 G-AXDH was kept at Blackbushe Airport, just a few miles north of Farnborough, and the team were based at the Parachute Regiment HQ in nearby Aldershot.

Alongside the main A325 road, between Farnborough and Aldershot, lies a 90-acre open, grassy space. This is known as Queen's Parade. It is owned by the MoD and it is so named because it was here that Queen Victoria carried out her annual review and inspection of the personnel of the Aldershot garrison. In the nineteenth century the area was also used for horse racing. A hundred years later, on weekdays in the 1970s, a large silver-grey, tethered balloon could often be seen hovering over the area at around 1,000ft; it looked like an overfed, bulbous bird of prey. Beneath its rotund belly was suspended a cage, from which new recruits to the Parachute Regiment would make their initial earthward plunges. Their parachutes were activated by a static line tied to the cage and would open after they had fallen about 100ft. The balloon could take about half a dozen of these Brave Young Men aloft at a time; hence it would spend its day being winched up and down until the supply of BYM had been exhausted.

At weekends and by special arrangement, the Red Devils' aircraft could use the 900m stretch of grass parallel with the road for take-off and landing. This meant that training sorties for the team, prospective team members and other service personnel could be completed within a stone's throw of the barracks and HQ.

I made my first foray to Queen's Parade on Sunday, 27 August 1978 to meet Captain Murray – he wasn't an Army captain, but an airline pilot with British Airways – so was a real 'captain speaking'! It turned out that his day job was flying Concorde, so flying the Islander was something completely different. After Dave had introduced me, we got on with the mission of the day, which was to get me signed up as an Islander pilot. I already had twin and instrument ratings on my civil licence, so this would be a type rating test.

My preparations with the flight manual paid off and we were soon ready to taxi to the downwind end of the parade and turn towards the south-west. Before I increased the power, Captain Murray pointed out a gap in the trees on the far edge of the grass, about 800m away. He said that I should aim towards that if I ever lost an engine after take-off, when it was too late to land back on and stop. At that point I remembered reading that the single-engine rate of climb would be about 150ft per minute, so I might need to use the gap! However, I was expecting to have a ground roll of about 300m, so we should be off the ground well before the trees. Even on that warm summer's afternoon we were airborne quite quickly and soared over the trees safely; then I remembered that there were just the two of us on board. *It might be quite different with a dozen beefy paratroopers and their kit*, I thought.

Up and away the little airliner flew and, apart from needing a modicum of rudder with aileron to balance the roll when turning, it performed as advertised. The stall behaviour was unremarkable with the minimum stall speed with flaps down of 40kt; a beeping stall-warner cut in about 5kt before the stall. It was sufficiently annoying to get one's attention easily. Captain Murray put me through my paces by getting me to fly around with only one engine producing thrust and he showed me how to react to the instructions from the 'jumpmaster' as the aircraft approached the drop-point. After a few circuits at Blackbushe we returned to Queen's Parade for a final landing. There were no runway markings on the grass so it was just a question of choosing the touchdown spot and aiming for it, estimating an approach path angle of 3–4 degrees. With the flaps fully down, an approach speed of 55–60kt was safe and, once the throttles had been closed and the aircraft held in the landing attitude, the stall warning beeper sounded just before the wheels contacted *terra firma*. Stopping was easy, the brakes were very effective and we stopped after about 150m.

The next time I flew from Queen's Parade was a couple of weeks later, with Dave Peet in the other seat to help me, as I did my first few parachute drops. These were of a selection of folk doing jumps from various heights aiming at the circle on the grass below. We had to work with Heathrow radar to make sure we didn't get in the way of any real airliners inbound to London's airports. After climbing to the altitude required by the jumpmaster I had to use my map to find the drop zone (DZ) and turn towards it. It was preferable to make the drop track into wind so I had already made sure we were downwind of the DZ. On the run-in the jumpmaster gave directions; it was my job to follow those calls, turning by using a combination of rudder and aileron to make the small adjustments using the minimum amount of bank angle. It was all very similar to the medium-level bombing I had done in my RAF training. Sometimes, and especially for free-fall drops, a wind marker would be dropped when over the DZ; this was a cylinder with a multi-coloured streamer attached to it. I had to stay on heading until its landing point had been noted. This then gave the jumpmaster an idea of how far beyond the DZ he would get the parachutists out.

The next part of the procedure was to turn downwind and repeat the set-up. But this time it would be bodies leaving the aircraft instead of the wind marker. An added job for me during the 'live' run was to throttle back the port engine just before the drop, so reducing the turbulence and slip-stream on the side from which the crazy people jumping out of a perfectly serviceable aeroplane would leave. After dropping several loads of temporary passengers I felt that I'd got the hang of it.

That was good because my next job was to take the aircraft to Barton airfield, a few miles west of Manchester; once there I had to refuel it and then find my way to a hotel for the night. The team would arrive the next morning and we would take-off from Barton and fly to Wrexham in North Wales for a free-fall drop into the football ground. I drew lines on maps, looked up all the radio frequencies I would need, checked that the warning notice for our adventure had been promulgated and then made sure that the aircraft was ready to go. I had flown up the previous day with the large left side door in place. Now it had to come off and be loaded onto the coach that had brought the team up and would take them home again. That meant that I would have a draughty trip back to Blackbushe!

There was only one new thing for me to do on this, my first team drop, and that was to fly past, behind the team as they lined up for the salute to the crowd. I had quizzed the team leader, Captain Mickey Munn, about this. How low should I be? How long from last man out to you all being lined up? If this is a football ground, will there be people on all sides? And if so, which direction are you going to face? He provided all the answers, so I now had no excuse. I had only a vague idea how I was going to get down from the drop height of 12,000ft and fly by at just the right time! But with an 'it'll be alright on the night' outlook I started up with my load of twelve red bodies and we set off. One surprise was that the cabin was so packed that there was a para sitting next to me in the cockpit. I wondered how he would catch up with the others when they all rushed out of the door.

Even with a full fuel load we were within our maximum weight limit, based on an estimate of 200lb per Red Devil, but without the door and seats. However, the take-off from the grass runway was as bumpy as at Queen's Parade but a lot longer. I talked to Manchester Airport radar as we climbed and headed south-west. About twenty minutes later we were in sight of the town and I picked out the green square of the football ground, so I headed to a point about 5 miles downwind of it. As I turned into wind for the first approach for the marker drop the chatter from the back subdued and the jumpmaster's voice came into my headset. Things then went as planned and on our second run, the 'throttle back!' call was followed by the noise of twelve grown men rushing and pushing to fall out of the door. The young man next to me slipped over the back of the co-pilot's seat with a shout of farewell (or was it 'Geronimo!'?). It went very quiet for a second or two and then the draught, heretofore blocked by the many large bodies, blew around the back of my neck.

I banked hard to the left, frantically searching the sky below me for falling bodies with smoke coming from their feet, while simultaneously throttling back the engines and stuffing the nose down. I spotted the team as they joined up and, keeping them in sight, I made a wide circle around them. I had caught them up just as their parachutes opened so now I had to get down low and position myself north-west of the DZ on the football ground. Mickey was going to line them up facing the main stand, which was on the south-west side of the pitch. I saw the parachutes collapsing as I turned in with a couple of miles to run; I hoped that my timing was OK. I was allowed to descend to 200ft over the ground so I swooped down to fly past. As I banked right to see how the team were doing I spotted the last man getting into line. Result! I climbed immediately after the fly-by with full power, turned left and set a heading for Blackbushe at 2,000ft.

For the rest of the season I flew more such display sorties, plus training days and some charity drops from the charmingly named Halfpenny Green airfield near Wolverhampton. In October I was the team pilot for four days of the British Motor Show at the National Exhibition Centre (NEC) near Birmingham. A few days before it was due to start, I flew, with Mickey Munn, to Birmingham Airport, which is but a hop, skip and jump from the NEC. At the airport I arranged refuelling and overnight parking for DH and discussed with air traffic control the best routines for operations in and out of the airport and the use of the very busy airspace for parachuting. Free-falling from 12,000ft in the busy Birmingham Control Area was not going to be easy to co-ordinate. We also visited the NEC to look at the DZ, which was a grass area on the edge of the main exhibition site. It was not very big – 'bijou' Mickey called it – and it was surrounded by huge floodlight masts; I estimated them to be at least 150ft tall. As Mickey examined the 'arena' I looked at the lines I could take for the flypast that would avoid the masts.

In all we were there for four days and did several drops. Sadly, the cloudy weather limited all the displays to lower levels and one had to be called off after we found the cloud base to be below team limits. That led to another new experience. Usually with the guys down the back I could hear their banter and joshing in the background over the radio chat. But when I was told that they were not going to jump and I was asked to do a low flypast at the DZ, it went much quieter. I positioned to fly across the DZ, as I had for the previous successful drops. As we did so two or three of the guys stuck their feet out of the door and ignited their smoke flares. We flew past the crowd like a single, slow Red Arrow, with multi-coloured smoke coming from the back end! Then it went even quieter when I set up to land at Birmingham – not a sound from the back.

I asked Mickey about it later. 'Well, they were a bit nervous – they're not used to landing in aeroplanes; they don't do it very often!' he said.

A couple more display venues rounded off the year and, as I was posted from Farnborough at the end of 1978, that was the end of my brief spell as a parachute display team pilot. Although not traditional air display flying, a lot of the work in the preparation and execution was similar. Liaison with display operators, following airspace regulations, knowing the aircraft's limits and operations manual and, most importantly, knowing when to go and when to stop, were all common factors regardless of the display routine. It was all good experience that would come in very handy in the future.

Part 2

SKYWRITING

4

Blackburn B-2

This part of the book is not about taking to the skies with smoke generators and writing words for all below to marvel at and read. That's an aviation activity I have never done, although as a RAF student pilot I did once try to write my initials in the sky with a condensation trail! Proper skywriting as a publicity practice became relatively common in the inter-war years; indeed, S.E.5a F904 (G-EBIA) that I flew later followed its First World War service with a brief spell operating in that commercial role. Rather, in the context of this book, the title refers to some aviation journalism with which I became involved in the late 1970s. This venture into writing articles for aviation magazines resulted from an encounter at the 1978 Farnborough Airshow with a professional journalist called Peter Gilchrist.* Although I had an innate wariness of members of the media, Peter impressed me with his enthusiasm for and knowledge of all things aviation. It also became quickly

---

*   See *Trials and Errors* (p.182) by this author; published by The History Press, 2015.

obvious that, unlike some hacks, he was a stickler for getting his facts right. He suggested that we might collaborate on a series of articles in which I would fly various interesting aircraft types and give a summary of their handling and performance. He already had good contacts with a couple of titles, including Ian Allan's *Aircraft Illustrated*. After he had received the go-ahead from Ian Allan, our first venture was to the north of England to fly the 1930s-era Blackburn B-2.*

The sole remaining Blackburn B-2 in flying condition was then operated by British Aerospace at the aeroplane's birthplace – Brough in Humberside.** The B-2 was regularly displayed at airshows by two nominated BAe pilots. One of these was Don Headley, the BAe chief test pilot for the Buccaneer and Phantom, based at nearby Holme-on-Spalding-Moor – always referred to as HOSM. I had known Don for more than three years and he readily agreed to my proposed visit to fly the B-2 with him.

The B-2's progenitors were a series of light, biplane trainers with the name Bluebird. The first Bluebird was Robert Blackburn's entry for a 1924 Air Ministry competition for lightweight, two-seat training aircraft; Blackburn was its designer and builder. Sadly, the Bluebird was unable to compete because it was so underpowered that, despite its lightweight wood and fabric structure, it could not meet the entry conditions. But gritty Yorkshireman Mr Blackburn, who had been building successful flying machines since 1909, wasn't going to let that stop him. Moreover, he knew that a successful training aircraft might lead to lucrative production and support orders; the thought of a profit will always urge a Yorkshireman on!

The Bluebird differed from most other trainers of the 1920s in that the two seats were arranged side-by-side, rather than in tandem. Blackburn believed strongly that this enhanced the effectiveness of pilot training and was a more sociable way to fly in those open-cockpit, pre-intercom days. So he persevered with improvements to the design. Over the next seven years the installation of an 80hp engine and the introduction of a metal fuselage, instead of wood and fabric, made the Bluebird the aeroplane of choice for many civilian flying clubs as well as individual customers. In 1930 a Blackburn Bluebird became the first light aircraft to circumnavigate the globe, in the capable hands of a redoubtable aviatrix – the Hon. Mrs Victor Bruce.

---

* The original article appeared in *Aircraft Illustrated*, February 1979.
** The B-2 is now housed with and operated from the Shuttleworth Collection at Old Warden aerodrome in Bedfordshire.

By 1931 no fewer than seventy-nine Bluebirds had been built and were in use with flying clubs and military reserve training schools. Blackburn was now experienced in the use of metal alloys in aircraft design and production, so he decided to make changes to the Bluebird that would take it out of the civilian marketplace and place it in competition with de Havilland and Hawker for a military trainer. This redesigned Bluebird became known as the Blackburn B-2. Blackburn argued that the enhanced durability arising from the B-2's increased strength and ruggedness would offset the greater capital cost. To cope with the additional weight he installed a 120hp engine.

Forty-two B-2s were built at Brough between March 1932 and February 1936, most of them serving with the Blackburn-owned flying schools at Hanworth, Middlesex, and at Brough itself. The aircraft formed the nucleus of the Elementary Flying Training Schools established at both locations by the RAF. However, the Air Ministry was officially critical of the B-2's side-by-side seating arrangement and chose the tandem DH Tiger Moth as the RAF's primary trainer. The only known direct competitive fly-off between the two types took place in, of all places, Lisbon. Once more the Tiger Moth came out as the winner and was chosen as the Portuguese Air Force's basic trainer. Nevertheless, the B-2 continued to serve as an elementary trainer alongside its rivals throughout the 1930s, training thousands of civilian and military pilots: pilots who would be sorely needed before the end of the decade.

Let's now return to Brough in the late 1970s and to two pilots walking towards an attractive little biplane, shining like a new pin and offsetting the matt grey finish of the sky above. Don Headley showed me round the pretty aeroplane, the shiny metal finish trimmed with light blue wing struts and registration letters – G-AEBJ. The B-2 has a wingspan of 24ft and a fuselage length of 30ft; the top wing, containing the fuel tank, is 9ft off the ground. As we walked around, Don showed off his vintage pride and joy, pointing out the neat cooling air vents behind the engine cowlings, the Handley Page slats on the outer leading edges of the upper wing and the relatively advanced shock-absorbing undercarriage.

We climbed into the cosy, sparsely equipped cockpit; I sat on the left – the student pilot's seat. The 1930s ambience had been well preserved in here, too. Varnished wooden floor, basic seats with Sutton harnesses and the antique instruments in the small neat instrument panel all spoke of the era. We confirmed with the man outside that the fuel tap in the fuel line from the tank above our heads was open, the ignition switches were off, and that the throttle was closed. He turned the propeller a few times and then put it in the desired position for starting. He stuck his thumb up. I switched the ignition switches on and set the throttle about an inch open.

'Contact!' I called.

He pulled on the prop and, with a crack and a pop, the engine fired and started to turn over smoothly at about 1,000rpm. I checked that the oil pressure had risen and, as there was no cylinder head temperature gauge, I waited a few minutes before I opened the throttle to check the magnetos were operating correctly, before waving the chocks away. We trundled across the grass towards the start of the take-off strip. I found it quite difficult to turn as the tailskid didn't seem to grip the grass; I needed bursts of power to give life to the rudder and make the little aeroplane go where I wanted it to. The B-2 had no brakes so the bursts of power had to be brief to keep the speed under control. As I moved across the airfield I was very impressed by the view ahead; it was much better than comparative contemporary trainers, such as in the Tiger Moth. I noted where the horizon cut across the nose: this was the three-point attitude that I would need on landing.

At the take-off point I checked the elevator trim setting on the rather odd, hockey stick-shaped lever. Throttle friction tight, fuel on, engine instruments OK, harnesses tight and locked and elevator and aileron controls full and free. I applied full throttle. The 120hp Gipsy engine barked and off we went. There was a very slight swing to the right, but it was very easy to control; the rudder was now effective in the slipstream. A small push on the stick readily brought the tail up. Soon after, at 55mph, with a small rearwards stick movement, the B-2 was airborne. It was in trim and I climbed away at 60mph; timing the initial climb gave a very respectable 600ft per minute (about the same as a Chipmunk). The engine was running at just over 2,000rpm.

During the flight I found that while the handling and control in pitch was good, just what you would want for a trainer, laterally and directionally it was a bit lacking – but typical of the times. There were two ailerons on the lower wing, so roll power was not what it could have been, with two more on the upper wing. However, the worst aspect was a bad case of what's called rudder overbalance. This means that the rudder once deflected then goes to full travel with no further input from the pilot. American test pilots will call this misbehaviour 'rudderlock'. Whatever you call it, it is highly undesirable, but again it was not unusual in aircraft of that period. For instance, de Havilland had installed a bungee centring spring in the rudder circuit to alleviate this bad behaviour on their Tiger Moth.

I noticed that while I was flying, Don had his feet on a set of footrests above his rudder pedals. I thought that this was a novel and useful feature and wished that a set had been provided for me when I was instructing!

We next set up for a test of the B-2's stalling characteristics. After looking out all around and making sure that all in the cockpit was as it should be, I closed the throttle, countered the slight yaw to the left with the rudder and let the aircraft decelerate. The B-2's behaviour was conventional for a trainer, with a crisp, straight, nose-down stall at about 37mph, after a light but noticeable buffeting felt at 2–3mph before the stall itself. Recovery using forward movement of the stick and full throttle was prompt and easy to fly; the little aeroplane lost about 200ft in altitude during the whole manoeuvre.

Don said that we should head towards HOSM and once overhead he took control to practise his aerobatic airshow sequence. Down below it was lunchtime and he knew that air traffic services were shut down, so no one should get in our way. Anyway, he was up here so he couldn't be flying a Buccaneer or a Phantom! I could see that there were groups of people walking about the site and the firemen were playing volleyball near their gaudy vehicles. As we puttered into earshot, pale faces turned upward and all activity stopped, everyone pausing to enjoy the quiet nostalgia evoked by the appearance of the shiny, veteran flying machine. We could almost hear the 'Ahhs'!

Don took advantage of his appreciative audience and went into his airshow routine. He flew loops, barrel rolls, stall turns and wingovers, all in a speed range of 40 to 120mph. After his neat, well-positioned sequence Don handed me control and invited me to continue in similar vein. I noticed that he had avoided negative G, so I resolved to do the same. During the aerobatics I confirmed my earlier impression that the lateral stick forces with large deflections were surprisingly heavy and the ensuing rate of roll was disappointingly low and needed a good dollop of rudder to help. However, in my experience of similar types of the era, this was fairly typical. The stick force per G when pulling into vertical manoeuvres was about 6lb; quite heavy for a light trainer. The B-2 was certainly no Stampe or early Pitts, a lot less lively than it looked – but still great fun!

The singing of the wind in the wires, the ever-changing airflow across the cockpit and the sight of the ground, with all those upturned faces, swinging around and over us combined to create that unique magic that only comes with an open cockpit. The sheer delight of flying a unique and good-looking vintage biplane under these conditions leads you right into the Nostalgia Trap, where flight testing becomes less of a science and more of an emotional experience.

Before we dropped down for a few circuits, we climbed to a safe height so that I could try a spin. The entry, three turns and recovery were all unremarkable – the B-2 fulfilled all the requirements as a trainer. However, the rudder lock made the forces on the rudder pedals seem to reverse – so that might be a drawback.

Throttling back to idle and flying at 60mph gave us a descent of about 500ft/min and I positioned us downwind for a circuit using the grass strip at HOSM. I flew the curving final approach at 60mph and reduced to 50 as we approach the touchdown point, where I closed the throttle and flew as low as possible until I had pulled the nose up to the three-point attitude, when I just held everything steady and the little B-2 settled on the wheels and skid. Result! What impressed me most was the view ahead throughout. I could see over the nose until the last few seconds; there really is no comparison in a tandem two-seater such as the Tiger Moth, in which you fly solo from the back seat. That layout requires the pilot, often an *ab initio* student, to guess the way ahead using clues gathered from each side of the nose. The B-2 was easy to fly around the circuit and only a little less easy to land successfully.

So what did I learn about Mr Blackburn's B-2? The first thing was that I wondered why it hadn't 'caught on' in the 1930s: was it the price or was it the military mindset that wanted a 'single-seat' cockpit environment for the student to learn in? Much later I became peripherally involved in the choice of a new RAF basic trainer to replace the side-by-side Jet Provost. The competition uncovered a strong lobby for the 'single seat environment' and against another side-by-side cockpit. *Plus ça change, plus c'est la même chose*!

Moreover, a basic trainer has a fixed position in the career of a student pilot. It acts as a filter and, like little Shetland ponies, exists to knock the ragged edges off before the student is allowed to handle a thoroughbred. It must have good handling qualities but it also needs a little spirit and even a bit of meanness. Perhaps the B-2 was just too well-mannered and too easy to fly for the RAF to use it successfully for selecting eager, but perhaps anxious, future Hind, Gladiator, Hurricane and Spitfire pilots?

5

Boeing B-17 Flying Fortress

BOEING B-17 'SALLY B'

By the beginning of September 1979 Peter Gilchrist and the publisher had arranged for me to fly the famous Boeing B-17G Flying Fortress *Sally B*.[*] To say that I was excited was a considerable understatement! *Sally B* is the name of a 1945-built B-17G and she is the only airworthy B-17 left on this side of the Atlantic. She has flown at countless airshows in the UK and across Europe, as well as serving as an airborne memorial to the USAAF airmen who lost their lives in the European theatre during the Second World War. This aircraft was delivered to the USAAF on 19 June 1945 as 44-85784, too late to see active service in the war, struck off charge in 1954 and bought by the French Institut Géographique National for use as a survey aircraft. In 1975 she was acquired by Ted White, moved to England and was registered with the CAA as G-BEDF to be restored by Ted's company, Euroworld. In 1981 Ted was killed in an air accident in Malta and since then

---

[*] The original article was published in *Aircraft Illustrated*, December 1979.

his partner, Mrs Elly Sallingboe, after whom the aircraft is named, has kept the operation going.*

The Boeing B-17 Flying Fortress is a four-engine heavy bomber developed in the 1930s for the US Army Air Corps (USAAC). Competing against Douglas and Martin for a contract to build 200 bombers, the prototype Model 299/XB-17 outperformed both competitors and exceeded all the required specifications. Although Boeing lost the contract because the prototype crashed, the USAAC ordered thirteen more B-17s for further evaluation. From its introduction in 1938, the B-17 Flying Fortress evolved through numerous models, becoming the third most produced bomber of all time.

The B-17 was primarily employed in the daylight strategic bombing role; its missions complemented the RAF's night-time area bombing. The B-17 also participated to a lesser extent in the Pacific theatre, where it conducted raids against Japanese shipping and airfields. From its pre-war inception, the USAAC, which became the US Army Air Force (USAAF) in June 1941, promoted the aircraft as a strategic weapon. It was a relatively fast, high-flying, long-range bomber with heavy defensive armament. It soon developed a reputation for toughness and an effective bomber, dropping more bombs than any other US aircraft in the Second World War. Of the 1.5 million tonnes of bombs dropped on Nazi Germany and its occupied territories by US aircraft, 640,000 tonnes were dropped from B-17s.

The final outcome of the negotiations between the magazine publisher and the owner and operator of *Sally B* was that I would meet up with the B-17 display team at Duxford** airfield, near Cambridge, on Saturday, 7 September 1979. The aircraft was due to display that weekend at the annual Battle of Britain Open Day at RAF Finningley near Doncaster, in South Yorkshire. I would be allowed to handle the aircraft on the outbound leg, but not allowed to fly the take-offs or landings. As the saying goes – beggars can't be choosers. I was just going to have to do as much assessment as I could en route and observe carefully for the rest of the time. The story starts when I arrived at Duxford early that day.

---

*   In 2008, Elly Sallingboe was awarded the Transport Trust's Lifetime Achievement Award in recognition of more than thirty years of dedication to the preservation and operation of Britain's only airworthy Boeing B-17 Flying Fortress as a flying memorial to the tens of thousands of American aircrew who lost their lives in her sister aircraft during the Second World War.

**   Duxford is the home of many historic aircraft operators and part of the British Imperial War Museum.

The morning mists of an early September morning were clinging damply to the grass, a limp windsock and my hair. I walked towards the flight line and looked expectantly ahead. Luminous grey ghosts loomed silently and morphed into spectral aeroplane shapes alongside the dark bulk of a hangar. Perspective, shape and size were all confused by the sparkling greyness swirling around in the crisp, autumnal air. Out across the tarmac apron, a looming silhouette commanded my attention more than the fantasia of historic aviation surrounding me. I walked on and it took on more detail. Four huge radial engines jutted purposefully from the leading edges of wide, thick wings. The metal and Plexiglas nose reared more than 10ft above me as the beast sat peacefully on its tailwheel and two fat mainwheels; I stopped in my tracks to admire its dangerous beauty. As I stood there, in something approaching awe, the mist shifted, patches of blue sky appeared in the whiteness above me and sunlight started to split the clouds.

Suddenly there was a movement: the small rear door on the B-17's fuselage opened. In the ambience that had built up around me I fully expected to see a bedraggled but boisterously relieved crew of ten American aircrew spill out noisily onto the wet grass. But I soon remembered that this was Duxford in 1979 not Bassingbourn, Bovingdon or Bury St Edmunds in 1944. I was here for a unique flying experience.

The sole figure that dropped from the door turned out to be one of the team engineers, Pete Smith. After introductions, which elicited the satisfying news that my arrival was expected, he said that there would be a bit of a wait before the pilots arrived and we would depart northwards. So I asked him if I could take a look around, inside and outside the aircraft; he was happy as long as I stuck to the usual rule of not moving any levers or switches.

In contradiction of the old proverb that you can't tell a book by its cover, a critical look at an aeroplane can tell you a lot about it. The broad, thick, 104ft span wing was obviously designed that way to lift more than 30 tons of flying machine over long distances and at relatively low airspeeds. The B-17 cruised at an indicated airspeed of around 180mph and operational altitudes of 25,000–30,000ft; its maximum range with a 6,000lb bomb load was around 1,780 nautical miles (nm). The four, big, round Wright Cyclone R-1820-97 radial engines bulged with potential power, which would be translated into thrust by 11ft 7in, three-bladed Hamilton variable pitch props. Each nine-cylinder, turbocharged engine could produce 1,200hp. Although now stripped of its chin, upper, waist and unique ball gun positions (when it was modified by the French), the elongated cigar of the all-metal, monocoque fuselage still exuded an air of rugged purposefulness.

A closer look at a few of the external details revealed some of the contemporary technology used by Boeing in its creation. There were the multi-bladed turbine discs mounted externally on the underside of each engine nacelle; these were the drive elements of the exhaust gas-powered superchargers. The single skin split flap spanned more than 24ft of each wing trailing edge. There was also evidence of the expanding rubber 'boots' for de-icing the wings in flight and very neat slots in the wing behind each engine for the egress of the engine-cooling air.

Before I boarded for a look around inside, another engineer, John Littleton, arrived and Pete Smith and I gave him a hand turning over each propeller nine times to make sure that no oil was pooled in the lower cylinders. Starting with that condition could seriously damage the engine. Once we had recovered from the considerable physical effort, I made my way to the tail end to enter by the rear door.

Once aboard I could see aft towards the now unused rear gunner's position. Access to that lonely eyrie would not have been easy as the large jack, strut and fairing of the tailwheel was in the way. Tail gunners in B-17s must have been a special breed, because once there it would have been virtually impossible to return to the door in flight, especially in the bulky, often electrically heated, clothing needed for those ten-hour missions at 30,000ft. Fortunately, the rear gunner had his own emergency exit under the starboard tailplane.

Turning to face forward, I found the unexpected sight of five airliner-style seats in what was once the waist gunners' compartment. These incongruous but useful modern additions are for transporting the Euroworld support team with their aircraft in a modicum of comfort. I moved on further forward and into what was once the radio compartment. As I did so a sense of history pervaded the air. Although this B-17 had never seen 'action', I could feel all around me the ghosts of hunched figures in heavy, sheepskin flying jackets, baseball caps and oxygen masks, Ahead of this compartment was a dark section, beyond which I could see the flight deck. As I stepped over the bulkhead into this dark space I spotted that there was no floor, just a 9in-wide metal plank. Two ropes formed a slack handhold on each side of this precarious path; I realised that I was now in the bomb bay. The bomb doors were clearly discernible in the dusty gloom below my feet. The bombs would have been stacked vertically on each side of the bay. The space itself seemed small in comparison with the vast hole underneath some of the RAF bombers – especially that of the Lancaster. That was why the B-17's maximum bomb load was just 6,000lb – which could be made up of a variety of ordnances from 100lb to 2,000lb bombs; although, due to loading limitations, it could only carry two of the latter.

I completed my rather perilous journey across the void and entered the cockpit – or more correctly perhaps, the flight deck. Previously I had only seen films of the interior of the B-17's front office, usually with Steve McQueen, or some other gritty hero, struggling with the controls; all the while chewing gum or smoking a cigar – sometimes both – and yelling commands at his crew!* As I stepped over the bulkhead out of the bomb bay I was struck by the narrow length of the cockpit area. The flight engineer's position was on the left and a table and radio racks were on the right; probably the navigator's position. The forward upper gun turret would have been above my head; it was operated by the engineer in combat. The long windows extended each side of the flight deck, well aft of the pilots' seats.

Ahead of them there was still 10–12ft of bomber! I found the access hatch to the nose section under my feet. I lifted the door, latched it to the side of the co-pilot's seat and ducked down under the throttle quadrant. Once through, I found myself in a large, airy, conical 'room'. All the major operational equipment had been removed, but this was where the bombardier would have used his Norden bombsight, linked through the autopilot, to control the big bomber on its final run to the target. He would concentrate all his efforts on achieving the correct release point, almost oblivious to the surrounding flak, fighters and associated mayhem, all too easily seen through the huge Plexiglas nose cone. Those last few minutes of a bomb run must have seemed like hours to the rest of the crew, especially to the temporarily redundant pilots.

With these thoughts I returned to the flight deck and climbed into the left-hand captain's seat. I adjusted it for height and noticed that it didn't move fore and aft. However, the enormous, pendulous rudder pedals could be adjusted individually to compensate.

The simple fabric-covered flying control surfaces were operated by a half-wheel control yoke and those big rudder pedals. There was no hydraulic boost, so I would expect control forces to be heavy, especially at higher

---

★ Steve McQueen played B-17 pilot Captain Buzz Rickson in the 1962 British film *The War Lover.*

speeds. Each control had its own trimmer, operated by wheels in the cockpit. That for the ailerons was to the left of the seat pan; it was not easy to move as there was a great deal of friction in the circuit. The nearby screw-jack indicator wasn't easy to see either. However, large changes in lateral trim were probably not a regular occurrence. The elevator trim wheel was conventionally placed alongside the pilot's right leg on the left side of the central pedestal. It was a smooth metal disc, had a little friction, but would have been easy to use. Its screw-jack indicator was easy to see and interpret. The rudder trimmer, however, although identical to the elevator trim wheel, was mounted in the floor athwartships, behind the central pedestal. It wasn't easy to reach and might have jeopardised control when it was needed, most probably after an engine failure. This was just one of the many factors of the cockpit design and mission of the B-17 that made two-man operation essential.

The rest of the flight deck was relatively conventional for its era. The large electrical control panel on the left testified to the prime mover of the B-17's systems: flaps, landing gear and bomb doors, as well as the gun turrets, autopilot, flight instruments, bombsight and many other subsystems. Sally B's instrument panels had been updated a little over the years but many of the primary gauges and dials looked original. The neat, space-saving trick of mounting all the engine instruments in pairs, with a numbered needle for each of the two engines, was new to me, but I liked it! Another panel space-saver was the fuel gauge. It had a single needle and an adjacent bakelite knob rotated the internal back plate of the dial as each tank was selected. Although hardly crowded, even more space was saved by not providing engine cooling cowl indicators. As the front of each engine was clearly in view it was only necessary to look out of the window to check the cowl setting.

At the bottom of the centre pedestal was the electronic autopilot; probably quite a rare fitting in the Second World War. It had about twenty different control knobs, each no doubt connected directly to a potentiometer; it must have been quite a handful to operate.

Above that were the fuel and engine control levers, the most striking of which were the throttles. The large three-bar gate arrangement dominated this part of the cockpit. At first I thought them overly large and ugly. *What was wrong with four smaller, neater side-by-side levers?* I thought. However, as soon as I got hold of them I took an instant liking to the arrangement. The central crossbar gave one-fist control of all four engines; dropping my hand to the lower crossbar gave control of the outer pair (Nos 1 and 4 engines) and the upper bar the inners (Nos 2 and 3). I eagerly anticipated checking out the use of this unusual configuration in the air.

And it wasn't long before that would be possible. The two pilots had now arrived. The captain was to be Don Bullock,* well known on the display circuit for his exciting displays in the B-17 and A-26 Invader. Don's day job was, and had been for some time, ferrying all sorts of aircraft around the world; he had been Euroworld's senior B-17 and A-26 pilot for about three years. His co-pilot was Chris Bevan, whose main occupation was as a British Airways Boeing 747 captain – a real case of 'Boeing Boeing'!

After introductions and the final agreement of when I would be allowed to pilot the aircraft, I followed Don and Chris, with Pete Littlejohn the flight engineer, up to the cockpit. The other support crew took their places in the comfy seats amidships. I took up station between the pilots as they got ready to start the engines. After the usual preparatory checks they shared the task of getting the aging Cyclones to show some sign of life. The start sequence was 3, 2, 4, 1; the inner engines being started first so that should one of them catch fire the groundcrew could access them with a fire extinguisher without having to avoid the whirling props of the outer engines. On each start Chris initiated the action by using the start switch to spin up the inertia starter flywheel, before using the mesh switch to transfer all that whirring energy to the appropriate powerplant. Don's simultaneous digital activity with the magneto switches, throttle and mixture levers eventually paid off as each motor burst into smoky life.

After all four motors were purring happily at 1,200rpm and the after start checks had been completed, Chris checked in with Duxford, received instructions and we set off towards the threshold of runway 26. As we taxied I noted that the view dead ahead was obstructed by the long nose. However, the view from about 10 degrees each side of the nose was excellent for a big, tailwheeled aeroplane. A slight increase in power on the outer engines had got us going and now we were moving along nicely with all four engines at a fast idle. Of course, we were more than 15,000lb lighter than an

---

* In July 1981 Don Bullock died when the Euroworld A-26 Invader he was flying crashed doing a barrel roll at the Biggin Hill airshow. There were seven people on the aircraft, five of whom were passengers. Following this tragedy the CAA tightened display regulations and banned pilots from displaying with anyone other than operating crew on board. The accident raised many more questions and a voluntary body, the Historic Aircraft Association (HAA) was formed to help with the self-regulation of the operation and display of historic and classic aircraft. I was the honorary secretary of the HAA for a while.

operationally loaded B-17G would have been thirty-five years earlier. As we taxied around the airfield, Don was using a combination of toe brakes and differential power on the outer engines to help us negotiate the corners; it all looked easy. However, the tailwheel lock had to be removed for cornering and relocked on the straight stretches. This job was the co-pilot's, using a lever on the floor to his left. A red light, near the single green landing gear down light, came on when he unlocked the tailwheel. Before lining up on the runway, Don checked each engine's magnetos, prop and supercharger controls at between 1,500 and 2,100rpm. With a sidelong glance at a slightly smoky No. 2 engine, a knowing smile and a wink from Pete Littlejohn, it was decided that all was 'GO' and we lined up on the runway.

Don smoothly applied full power, Chris followed up on the throttles and off we went. Although not quite in the same league of authority and noise as the Lancaster's Merlin engines, the surge of smooth radial power vibrated through *Sally B*. The tail came up readily and after a ground roll of just over twenty seconds we lifted imperceptibly into the air at 110mph. Chris reached forward to a fairly insignificant-looking switch, near the top of the instrument panel, and selected the gear up. After about fifteen seconds the little green light went out; but just to confirm this, the pilots each looked out below the inner engines to ensure that Mr Goodyear's excellent rubber tyres had disappeared. Don accelerated to 140mph and at 300ft Chris set climbing power of 35in manifold air pressure (MAP) and 2,300rpm. We had achieved about 46in and 2,500rpm on take-off. Flaps were not normally used during take-off and we had used about 1,000 yards of runway. That length would probably have been doubled at maximum take-off weight.

During the climb to 2,000ft for our transit Chris set the cowl flaps for optimum engine cooling and checked their positions visually. As he did so I looked out along the wings, stretching more than 50ft each side. Despite the turbulence from our passage through fair weather summer thermals, I noticed that the wings didn't flex at all. I later discovered that the riveted metal skin covered a skeleton of metal trusses and ribs whose design seemed to owe more to bridge building than aeronautical engineering. Whatever the case, it was a strong and rugged wing; testified by the many wartime incidences of B-17s staggering back with holes in them and making safe arrivals on friendly airfields. The rigidity of the wing may, in time, have set up stresses in the wing root area – but there weren't many B-17s that survived long enough to suffer from long-term, metal fatigue problems!

Don now eased his lithe frame out of his seat, while Chris flew the air-craft. Once I had strapped in I set to work. We were cruising at 180mph and 2,000ft. The engines were set at 1,800rpm and 29–30 MAP (about zero boost for Brits). I found that the aircraft was easy to control in pitch, with lighter stick forces than I had expected to change attitude. As the speed and altitude changed I re-trimmed and found the elevator trimmer quite high-gained – a small movement had a fairly powerful and rapid effect. But by slowing down and holding the trim change with the stick, rather than trimming, I could make a crude assessment of the B-17's longitudinal static stability. I would have expected a big bomber of the era to have been strongly stable, so giving large forces for small changes in airspeed. In fact, *Sally B* was relatively lightly stable; that is not to say that she was in the fighter class!

I slowed down to 150mph and tried some aileron and rudder inputs to look at the lateral and directional stabilities. A moderate steady sideslip, achieved with about a 100lb push on the rudder, showed that there was not very much roll with yaw; this is called dihedral effect and can be useful for correcting lateral disturbances with rudder. I only needed a small deflection of the control wheel to hold the wings level. By simultaneously releasing the yoke and rudder pedals she corkscrewed back to steady flight. This motion is known as the Dutch roll (so named after the rolling gait of speed skaters on frozen Dutch canals). Through these brief tests I came to the conclusion that the B-17 had been well-endowed with balanced lateral and directional stability and that holding a heading on a bombing run would, theoretically, have not been too difficult. In fact, the autopilot would have been doing that, unless a failure had occurred and the pilots had had to take over.

I wanted to move on to the more dynamic aspects – especially rolling this beast. To check *Sally B*'s maximum roll rate, I put her up in a 30 degrees bank to the left, applied full right wheel and timed the period until we were at 30 degrees bank to the right. Then to check for symmetry I did it the opposite way. For these rolls I put in 110 degrees of wheel deflection and a force of about 50lb: maximum effort. The aircraft rolled through 60 degrees in ten to twelve seconds, so giving a roll rate of 5–6 degrees per second; hardly impressive! I then tried it again, adding a push of about 100lb on the rudder pedal in the same direction. The result was an improvement in roll rate of only 1 degree per second.

As I pondered what this might mean operationally, I took time to look around. The view ahead, left and behind the wing was excellent; in fact, I could see the end of the tailplane behind me. The view from the co-pilot's seat should have been exactly the same. That meant that the pilots should have been able to see any incoming enemy aircraft as the gunners called them out. However, the view above was severely limited by the roof panel, so the gunners would have to cover that area. With those ideas in my head I decided to try some evasive manoeuvring and, with lots of effort, rolled to 50 degrees of bank to the left; that took about eight seconds. Once there I pulled to get *Sally B* turning and hold level flight. She pitched into the turn easily, I needed barely a 10lb force on the wheel to pull her round at nearly 2g; a very simple task with two hands. The G limit of 4 might have been quite easy to exceed – not that an accelerometer was fitted to check. But by limiting steep turn bank angles to 60 degrees then 2–3g would rarely be exceeded and, at combat speeds, the rate of turn would have been impressive for a big aeroplane. However, to reverse the turn took a great deal of physical effort and time; time during which the aircraft would have become a virtual sitting duck, rolling slowly but not changing direction, solving the fighter pilot's firing solution, but also giving the gunners a tricky, rotating platform from which to respond.

The mismatch of control and stability puzzled me. However, I had to take into account that *Sally B's* centre of gravity was probably a little further aft that a loaded operational Fortress. That would emphasise the lightness in pitch that I had found. I also had to recognise that I'd tested her at 2,000ft, not in the less dense air at 20–30,000ft, where the rate of roll would be much better due to lower roll damping: that is less air resistance to the rolling motion of that big wing.

Now it was time to look at the aircraft at its approach and landing speeds. So, with a nod of agreement from Chris Bevan, who had been enormously patient so far, I throttled back to 20in MAP and he lowered the landing gear. That had little noticeable effect on the trim. Once we were below the limit speed of 147mph, Chris selected the flaps to 15 degrees, then at 125mph to 25 degrees and at 120kt to the fully down position of 45 degrees. The first selection caused a small, but easily corrected, nose up change of longitudinal trim, but the rest had no trim effect, they just slowed us down. I adjusted the throttles to hold the speed at 100–110mph – a late final approach speed for our current weight; the rpm was set at 2,100. The aircraft felt less responsive in pitch than before and even lighter. Directionally she felt solid but the rate of roll at 100kt was still poor: about 4 degrees per second. I throttled back the right outboard engine and found that it was easy to correct the yaw it caused. However, it really was difficult to operate that awkwardly placed rudder trim wheel. But once I'd got it under control I thought that a three-engined approach and landing would probably not be that much different from a normal, four-engined arrival.

As I wasn't allowed to do a landing I performed a full power 'go around' using all four engines as Chris retracted all the bits hanging down. The excellent elevator and its trimmer made this an easy task and I levelled off back at 180mph, just in time to hand back to Don, who had returned to the flight deck as we were approaching our destination.

I moved to the engineer's position to observe the approach and landing. The final turn was flown at 120mph with the gear down and 30 degrees of flap, and we were lined up with Finningley's 9,000ft runway at 300ft. The flaps were then selected fully down and the speed allowed to trickle back to 100mph as we crossed the threshold. Then Don eased the throttles all the way back, kept the nose coming up as the speed reduced further and then, in the three-point attitude, we just waited. A couple of seconds later *Sally B* was back on the ground with barely a bump. The brakes were applied steadily and we slowed smoothly to a walking pace. Before long we had parked, cut the engines and disembarked. As we walked away I threw a long glance back over my shoulder. There she was, looking incongruous in the surroundings of a modern military airfield, a symbol of her time.

I reflected on my impressions of this legendary bomber. The B-17 was a favourite with its aircrews, especially the pilots. But it's a well-known fact that pilots are a partisan breed when it comes to defending their machine's flying qualities. As a test pilot you soon learn that; especially if those pilots had not flown many other similar types, so had little to compare it with. Maybe those heavy ailerons and wallowing roll rate were not that unusual in a heavy aircraft of the B-17's era. Perhaps no one had complained about its lateral handling? In essence the wings of the B-17G were the same as the prototype. The ailerons were simple slab controls with no aerodynamic balancing. They did move differentially (to reduce adverse yaw) but they weren't really big enough. The state of the art in-flight control technology in 1935 was such that some form of aerodynamic balancing could have been used to reduce the forces, but it seems that the demand wasn't there.

It must be remembered that before the advent of their Y1B-9A twin-engined bomber project of 1931 and their subsequent Model 247 airliner, Boeing had put nearly all their eggs in the light aircraft basket. Their in-depth experience of 100ft plus wingspan aircraft was hardly extensive; neither was that of the USAAC. However, the tactics employed by B-17s of the Heavy Bombardment Groups over Europe from 1941 was that of the mass formation. That meant that the need for individual evasive manoeuvres would have been rare, as survival was dependent on massive cross-cover from all those on-board guns. So was it the aircraft that dictated the tactic or did the tactic counter the need for change?

Whatever the answer, in many other ways the Flying Fortress was technologically advanced in its concept and design. When it graduated to war it was equipped to carry out the almost suicidal doctrine of strategic, daylight, pinpoint bombing by large, tight formations, able to put down huge amounts of explosive on relatively small target areas. But what endeared it most to its crews was its ruggedness. Repeatedly they saw their squadron and mess mates brought home on three, two and even one engine, or in aircraft with huge holes torn in them. They also saw them fall from formation, like huge dying geese, but still hang together long enough for their crews to escape. They were, on the whole, proud of the B-17 and I could now see the reasons why. After all, men that despise their aircraft don't go to all the trouble of painting emblems (of all sorts!) and giving affectionate and, sometimes, shocking, names to them. There was among those thousands of American airmen an *esprit de corps* that I like to think was brought about by an aeroplane, not an ideal.

This B-17, which I had now had the privilege to fly, albeit briefly, was one of the last of the line and is now a lasting, soaring memorial. It continues to fly, like so many veterans, not by the whim of a millionaire but by the hard graft and loving care of a team of dedicated folk, led by the desire to 'keep 'em flying'. Well done to Elly Sallingboe and everyone else on her team.

6

Harvard

NA HARVARD

Those of you who have read my book *More Testing Times** may recall that I regularly flew the North American Harvard in the late 1980s and early '90s, while I was serving at the Aircraft and Armament Experimental Establishment (A&AEE), Boscombe Down. Indeed, I became a Harvard check pilot and instructor, as well as having an interesting incident in which we, that is Harvard FT375 and I, experienced air combat with a heavy-load parachute in flight: we won! As I hope that you will read later, I also became a member of the Harvard Formation Team. But my first flight in a Harvard actually took place on Tuesday, 9 May 1978. That was the day that all the protocol had been put in place for me to visit A&AEE and fly the Harvard with Sqn Ldr Fred Stanford. Although I have described flying the Harvard in the previous book, I will distil what I wrote for Ian Allan's *Air Extra*, No. 22 (undated) here. At the time I had about 1,300 flying hours on

---

* Published in 2017 by The History Press.

propeller-driven, tailwheeled aircraft; however, never with anything more than 140hp up front.

First, a potted history of the aeroplane. The original 1935 North American Aviation Company design developed into the AT-6 Texan trainer and it was already in use in the USAAC when the Second World War started. The RAF and Royal Canadian Air Force bought some of the early models to use as advanced trainers – this model became known as the Harvard I. Later in the war, modified, licence-built Harvards from the Canadian Noorduyn Company were used for the British Commonwealth Air Training Plan – these were designated the Harvard IIB. More than 15,000 AT-6/Harvard aircraft would be built and they would serve with the air arms of more than sixty countries.

The Harvard is a monoplane with a tandem, two-seat layout; the cockpit being covered by a long metal-framed and glazed canopy, which is fitted with two sliding hoods. These allow entry and egress to and from each pilot's station; the student pilot occupying the front seat. The all-metal fuselage is just less than 30ft long and the low-mounted wing spans 42ft. The two retractable main landing gear wheels are raised by hydraulic pressure, but can be released and locked down by gravity. The split flaps are also hydraulically operated and hydraulic foot-operated mainwheel brakes are fitted. The castoring tailwheel does not retract in flight. The Harvard is powered by a Pratt & Whitney R-1340-AN-1 Wasp radial engine, which develops 600hp and drives a variable pitch propeller. The Harvard weighs in at around 5,500lb. So let's go back to May 1978 and a young(ish) test pilot arriving at the big hangar that was the home of the A&AEE's B (Heavy Aircraft) Test Squadron.

It was a misty morning with the promise of hazy sunshine and a brisk breeze from the north-east. I went into the hangar and found the B Squadron crewroom to meet up with Squadron Leader Fred Stanford. He had joined the RAF in 1943, a year before I was born, and had trained on Tiger Moths and Harvards before moving on to Vickers Wellingtons; he later became a flying instructor and served throughout the Second World War. He stayed in the RAF after the war and after two tours in the Far East, flying a variety of transport types, he eventually returned to the UK to fly the C-130 Hercules before moving to Boscombe Down, where, in addition to the Hercules and Harvard, he flew the Comet, Britannia, Andover and Bassett: quite a selection. The three Harvards at A&AEE flew photochase sorties for parachute development trials. All three were finished in an overall yellow colour scheme, with RAF roundels and military registrations.

After agreeing my flight plan, we strode out together towards Harvard IIB FT375, sitting conspicuously in the bright sunshine illuminating the huge apron outside the hangar. While Fred signed the aeroplane's technical logbook, I climbed into the front cockpit; he would do the external checks while I strapped in. We were sitting on Irving parachutes and there was a conventional four-point seat harness. I was very familiar with both, so I soon felt at home in the huge cockpit and looked around. I could see nothing ahead – just the large instrument panel. Adjusting the seat pan fully up didn't help much; I still couldn't see out properly but at least I could now see the top of the engine cowling. The apparently vast space in the cockpit reminded me of large Texan pilots, like John Wayne and a wonderful line from wartime ace Ginger Lacey's book. On learning to fly the huge Republic P-47 Thunderbolt fighter he was told that the best evasive action was to trim it into a dive at full power and then unstrap and run about in the cockpit!

After Fred had given me a guided tour of the cockpit he strapped into the back and we got down to business. I checked around the cockpit that all was as it should be. Now I had to apply the parking brake. I looked around for a meaty lever. But, after asking Fred where it might be, he directed me to a small, insignificant, black bakelite knob on the right-hand side of the main instrument panel. I pushed with my feet on the rather awkward, almost vertical, size 15 brake pedals before pulling and holding the knob, then releasing the pressure on the pedals. There was very little indication that the brakes were actually on. The only clue was that the little black knob was slack over about half an inch of its travel. Now to get the motor going. First supply it with fuel. I pumped with a lever on my left until the fuel reached the correct pressure, indicated on a gauge in front of me, and then primed the engine cylinders using the ubiquitous Kigass pump on the right. All ready. Radio on, throttle set about an inch open, ignition switches on and give the groundcrew the wind-up signal through the open canopy.

With a returned thumbs up I put the spring-loaded start switch to 'energise'. Immediately I heard the almost musical rising whine from the inertia starter unit's flywheel. Fred's practised ear picked the correct note (possibly G sharp) and on his command – 'Now!' – I moved the start switch to 'start'. The stored energy in the whirling flywheel transferred itself to the crankshaft of the Pratt & Whitney Wasp, the prop turned and the engine soon burst into smoky life, quickly settling down at a burbling 1,000rpm.

A quick check around – hydraulics, electrics, radios – and we called for taxi clearance. I closed the throttle and waved the chocks away.

Once they had gone and the groundcrew had given us a final wave-off, I released the parking brake by a quick stab on the pedals. An increase of power to about 1,200rpm got us moving and I checked the brakes before I turned onto the taxiway. Once rolling on the concrete, the Harvard needed very little power to keep it going; indeed some brake was needed to control the speed and help with weaving the nose from side-to-side so as to clear the area ahead, previously hidden by the big round motor. During those manoeuvres I could feel the aeroplane's definite tendency to overswing and perhaps generate a 'ground loop'; that's an uncommanded pirouette – it's both embarrassing and potentially damaging to the aeroplane. The castoring tailwheel, narrow-track mainwheels and weight at the back end all contribute to this potential problem.

When we arrived at the grass strip, alongside Boscombe's 10,000ft runway, I had to park into wind to complete the power checks. Moving off the concrete onto the grass was like riding a horse from a road into a field; the same feeling of a change to the correct environment. I set the parking brake on, held the stick hard back, mixture fully rich, rpm lever set to MAX and increased power to -2½psi. Then the rpm lever was exercised twice over its full range to check the operation of the prop's constant speed unit before increasing power to zero boost at about 2,100rpm for individual magneto checks. Then it was back to 1,200rpm to complete the rest of the pre-take-off checks in relative tranquillity. Trims set; throttle friction set; mixture fully rich; rpm lever at MAX; flaps up; *fuel ... where are the fuel gauges? ... ah, perhaps out on the wings like the Chipmunk? ... no ... ask Fred ... where? ... so that's where they live!* The Harvard's fuel tank gauges are down on the cockpit floor each side of the seat, each with its own light, switched from the central electrical panel (an essential item down there in the gloom!). They were indicating 40 gallons each; that was enough for about three and a half hours flying. The ambiguously marked rotary fuel tank selector cock on the left cockpit wall was on 'reserve'; I moved it to 'left' for take-off. I wondered how many students had erroneously selected 'off' in days gone by, with, at best, embarrassing consequences. Back to the pre-take-off checklist. Carburettor heating selected to 'cold'; flight instruments all set and checked; direction indicator (DI) aligned with the compass and uncaged; pitot heater on; engine temperatures and pressure all satisfactory and within limits; harnesses tight and locked; canopies closed and locked; and, finally, flying controls all checked for full, free and correct movement.

So, the moment had arrived. We called for take-off clearance and were asked to hold while the ETPS Lightning thundered by 50 yards to our right. Chalk and cheese came to mind! As the Lightning departed rapidly skywards, we were given clearance to go, with a left turn onto a westerly heading for our climb to 6,000ft. A stab on the brake pedals released the parking catch once more and I slowly opened the throttle. With the stick just forward of neutral we gathered speed and I kept my feet ready to correct any directional wanderings. When the throttled reached its halfway position, the engine was turning at 2,200rpm and +2½psi was indicated on the neatly coloured boost gauge. This setting was used as a sensible compromise between preservation and the need to get airborne before the end of the grass strip.

As soon as the tail came up, which happened readily at 30–40kt, I could see that the world ahead of us really did still exist! The view of the other end of the airfield was short-lived. There was just time to check the airspeed – 60kt – then I eased the stick back slightly and FT375 lifted into the air at about 85kt. As soon as we had clear separation from the ground I selected the undercarriage up and accelerated to the climbing speed of 100kt. Once there I reduced rpm to 2,000, set zero boost for the climb and turned left onto west.

My immediate impressions were of pleasant handling qualities and easy trimmability. The aircraft seemed longitudinally stable and I had no difficulty in keeping her going straight. However, these niceties were offset by noise, heat and that fundamental odour of hot, petrol-driven, reciprocating engines. I couldn't do much about the noise and smell, but I looked around for vents to blow cool external air on my face. After enquiring of Fred, he said that there weren't any such luxuries and then asked me to check that the cockpit heater was off – it was. Then I had a flash of inspiration: open my canopy! It's easily forgotten in these jet-powered days that some aircraft don't fall apart if the canopy is opened in flight! Instant and beautifully fresh air was immediately available, coupled with that feeling of being at one with the environment. The resemblance of the Harvard's long, enclosed canopy to a greenhouse is not just visual!

Even with the moderate power setting the aircraft was climbing comfortably at almost 1,000ft per minute. The view ahead was satisfactory, with the top of the nose just below the horizon. Just one third rudder trim was needed to keep the slip ball centred. A few turns showed me that the Harvard, like many of its contemporaries no doubt, suffered from adverse aileron yaw, caused by the differential drag from the up and down ailerons. There were aerodynamic tricks available to designers, even back in the 1930s, but most of them put their faith in a very cheap yaw stabilisation system – the Mk1 human pilot!

I levelled off at 6,000ft and allowed the aeroplane to accelerate to 120kt; when there I set -2psi boost and 1,800rpm. The noise quickly fell to a reasonable level and I closed my canopy. After several fore and aft stick inputs I determined that the Harvard possessed a good short-term and positive response, making it easy to make quick and accurate changes of attitude. The static stability in pitch was also positive; a pull force of 5–6lb was needed to hold a speed reduction of 20kt. By slowing to 100kt and releasing the stick I found that the dynamic stability was also positive; the aircraft recovered to its trimmed speed of 120kt after two roller-coaster cycles (known as 'the phugoid' in the trade!). Thus the Harvard was – and still is – a pleasant aircraft to fly because its longitudinal stability and handling qualities are so good.

I next wanted to examine the Harvard's lateral and directional stability and control. After a few rolls I discovered that the best rate of roll was about 35 degrees per second. That might not be anywhere near modern trainers but was probably similar to some of the operational aircraft for which wartime student pilots were being trained. Directionally the Harvard showed me nothing that would be a concern for training.

I had been briefed that, as I was not converting to the aircraft, I would not be allowed to spin it. But Fred told me that the spin characteristics were pretty conventional. An eight-turn spin would lose about 3,500ft of altitude, including the one and a half to two turns during the recovery, which would follow the standard spin recovery actions. However, I was allowed to stall the Harvard. After checking several items in the cockpit and looking out all around and below, I closed the throttle and held level flight. The first and most immediate impression was of sudden quietness, with the Wasp purring at a flight idle of about 1,500rpm. The second thing that I noticed was that a red light just above the airspeed indicator had illuminated. This was the undercarriage not lowered warning lamp that was operated by throttle position; it commanded my immediate attention, so does its job well.

The aircraft decelerated steadily and needed just a touch of rudder to keep it going straight. As I maintained height, the horizon began to vanish behind the nose and at 70kt a mild, low-frequency buffet was perceptible.

I found that roll control power had diminished markedly but the rudder was still effective in eliminating any sideslip. The aft stick force lightened slightly and the aircraft began to gently waffle earthwards. At 60kt, with the control column still not fully back, the right wing dropped sharply to about 60 degrees bank and the nose soon followed its lead. Moving the stick briskly forward and using rudder to stop the nose yawing off any further, I applied about half throttle to help us ease out of the ensuing dive.

After regaining the 500ft or so of height we had lost, I repeated the whole process with the undercarriage and flaps down and just a trickle of power. The result was very similar to the previous 'clean' stall, except that the ailerons were even less effective and the buffet and loss of lift occurred at about 10kt less airspeed. The wing drop was markedly quicker and directionally unpredictable. During these stalls I voiced the feeling that the aircraft would spin quite easily if it was mishandled at low speeds. Fred confirmed this and told me that all students of the period had to be fully competent at spin recoveries before they were allowed to perform solo stalling.

Sadly, for reasons of preservation, aerobatics were not permitted; this was a real disappointment. Fred told me that in days of yore the Harvard was a very nice aerobatic mount, especially in the looping plane. He said that, unlike some prop planes, it had no bias against which way it wanted to go in stall turns. He added that once you were yawing round the top you were committed; with all that up-front weight rotating round the centre of gravity the result was quite snappy! He said that slow rolls were quite tricky (aren't they always?) and a lot of forward stick was needed to keep the nose up when inverted.

Now it was time to head back. I throttled back a little and lowered the nose to hold 150kt for the descent. After being given clearance to join the Boscombe Down circuit pattern, Fred took over to make sure that I could identify the grass strip while he positioned us overhead at 800ft. Having got myself orientated properly, Fred demonstrated a full circuit and landing. We turned downwind at 800ft and 100kt, selected the wheels down, put the rpm lever to 'MAX', selected the flap to 20 degrees, checked fuel level and selection, harnesses tight and locked, and that two green lights had appeared on the undercarriage indicator. When the landing end of the grass disappeared under the wingtip Fred throttled back to achieve a descending turn at 85kt before selecting full flap. About one quarter throttle seemed adequate to keep the desired flight path angle. The result was a pleasant, unhurried descent with the touchdown point in view until the last 100ft or so. At this point the speed was gradually reduced by raising the nose and closing the throttle. At about 65kt the landing spot disappeared behind Messrs Pratt and Whitney's excellent reciprocating motor. As the aircraft reached the three-point attitude the outside world became a series of airfield objects rushing through the gap between that huge lump of machinery up front and the leading edge of the wing. I was left with the impression that everything would be just fine as long as the engine could see where we were going! We touched down smoothly on all three wheels and then Fred applied power, took off again and we climbed away. Now it was my turn; no pressure then!

After raising the wheels and flaps I climbed back to 800ft and turned downwind. Once there I throttled back to hold 100kt and 800ft and carried out the pre-landing checklist. At the end of the downwind leg I throttled back to a trickle of power and rolled into the final turn. A small tweak of nose-up trim helped to hold the speed at 85kt and we settled comfortably into the descent. I selected full flap about a quarter of the way round the turn, leaving me time to concentrate on speed and flight path. Everything looked good and there were encouraging noises from the back seat. But, more importantly, it felt right. After rolling out on the centreline of the strip, which had now disappeared from view again, I raised the nose to reduce the speed to 65kt and then held the three-point attitude. We were only a couple of feet from the ground as I saw the taxiway that marked the extreme end of the grass strip float by just beneath us. I closed the throttle and seconds later we bumped moderately gently onto the grass.

Once down I applied 2½psi boost and accelerated to get airborne again, ready to have another go. The Wasp burst rudely into life, producing lots of yaw and lift over the tail as I moved the stick forward. I sensed a sudden need for lots of rudder as bits of Wiltshire hurriedly reappeared over the nose and the aircraft bounced impetuously along on its mainwheels. The docile, pleasant creature that I had just flown round finals had instantly changed character and I now had to be firm and active on all the controls to make a respectable attempt at a controlled departure. Fred had kindly retracted the flaps, obviating the need to use more than 2½psi boost on roller landings, and we were soon airborne, accelerating away to 100kt as I fumbled for the hydraulic power selector and undercarriage levers.

We went on to do a few more circuits, each one a slight improvement on the last, until I began to really enjoy flying the aircraft and appreciate its agreeable and responsive nature. At least I was ready for the 'bucking bronco' mode on the roller landings and could therefore handle them a little more competently!

Unfortunately lack of time, already so generously given, prevented a look at the glide approach or practice forced landing. However, I felt sure that the Harvard's infinitely variable flap, plus the occasional use of sideslip, would help to make them a reasonably civilised business. Certainly the Harvard was sufficiently well-mannered and responsive to enable even the most average student to bring off the occasional accurate spot landing.

And so to the final circuit and landing. I was keenly aware of the ground-looping reputation of the Harvard so after landing I was careful not to relax too early. Following Fred's advice, I kept working the rudder, ready for even the slightest sign of an undemanded sideways movement of the tail end. Only a little judicious braking was needed to enhance the natural drag of the grass and so bring the aircraft down to walking pace before turning onto the taxiway. I imagined that a landing on a hard surface might be a totally different ball game, especially with a crosswind.

After my first flight in the Harvard I realised how well it had stood the test of time. The original design team clearly came up with a very successful formula. The aeroplane has pleasant and precise, if not crisp, handling qualities. Harvards and T-6s have flown in almost every climate in the world and their rugged construction has enabled them to survive the rigours of training tens of thousands of raw and possibly overenthusiastic student pilots. The aircraft would have been popular with students and instructors alike. After a Tiger Moth, what would any of them have made of that big enclosed cockpit, powerful radial engine, variable pitch propeller, brakes, flaps and a retractable undercarriage? But they would have soon found that the challenges were conquerable and would have overcome the problems associated with its power and weight. Not to say that none of them ground-looped, or flicked into spins from stalls. Many did those things, but those that made it through to their operational conversion units had cut their teeth on a 'real' aeroplane and become airmen in the true sense of the word.

Little did I know in May 1978 that I would not only fly the Harvard again but become a check pilot and, later, a member of a formation team with no fewer than five of them. This first acquaintance stood me in good stead for that and the many happy hours I spent sitting behind that growling 600hp engine; I ended up with almost 100 hours in that spacious, if sometimes draughty, cockpit!

Part 3

THE SHUTTLEWORTH COLLECTION

7

A Brief History

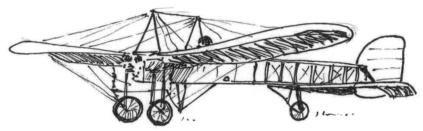

BLERIOT XI

The Shuttleworth Collection is a museum of vintage and veteran aircraft and motor vehicles, and is located at Old Warden airfield, near Biggleswade, south of Bedford in the English Midlands; most of the aircraft are still flyable and many of the vehicles driveable. They are all on view to the public throughout the year and regular flying displays are held. The Collection was founded in 1928 by aviator Richard Ormonde Shuttleworth. Following his death in 1940, his mother Dorothy formed the Richard Ormonde Shuttleworth Remembrance Trust 'for the teaching of the science and practice of aviation, and of forestry and agriculture'. The background history of the Collection goes back to the nineteenth century.

In 1842 the iron and steel business of Clayton & Shuttleworth was founded by Nathaniel Clayton and Joseph Shuttleworth; their foundry was in Lincoln. By 1845, they had produced their first portable steam engine and their first traction engine followed in 1858. They also produced a range of agricultural equipment that was exported widely. The wealth created by the company enabled Joseph Shuttleworth to buy Old Warden Park where, in 1872, a large, red-brick manor house was built. However, the current stone house replaced the brick one at some time in the early twentieth century.

Joseph's grandson, Richard Ormonde Shuttleworth, was born on 16 July 1909 at Old Warden and, at the age of 23, he inherited enough money to indulge his passion for motor racing and aviation. Richard purchased his first vintage car, an 1898 Panhard Levassor, which he subsequently drove in the London to Brighton Run. The car had previously taken part in the Paris–Amsterdam race. Around the same time he also bought his first aircraft, a DH.60X Moth (G-EBWD). Both the car and the aeroplane are still part of the Collection today.

Richard owned or drove a large number of cars including Bugattis, Alfa Romeos, a Railton, a 2.3-litre sleeve-valve Arrol-Aster, Rolls-Royces, and a vintage Jowett. He also enjoyed riding motorcycles and once owned a sleeve-valve Sparkbrook; he also owned and ran several steam-powered vehicles! Richard went on to have a successful motor racing career, which included winning the International Donington Grand Prix in 1935, driving his Alfa Romeo Monoposto. In January 1936 Richard went to South Africa for the East London Grand Prix. He was driving an Alfa Romeo, fitted with *de Ram* shock absorbers; however, he was not happy with the car's handling. Sadly, his concerns were realised when the Alfa Romeo left the road and he was seriously injured. Richard remained unconscious for nineteen days and didn't return to England until April; the accident ended his motor racing career.

After recuperating, Richard turned to aeronautics. He was particularly interested in historic aircraft and would track down abandoned aeroplanes, then restore them to pristine working condition in a workshop that is still in use at Old Warden. Richard first landed an aircraft at Old Warden on 26 September 1932, after a large field and its surrounds had been cleared of obstructing trees; that was the inauguration of today's aerodrome.

When the Second World War broke out Richard joined the RAF at Upavon for initial training. He did his main pilot course at RAF Ternhill and was awarded his wings on passing out from there. At RAF Benson he was on an operational training unit course and, after passing out, he was to be posted to Farnborough or Boscombe Down to join Alan Wheeler and work in accident investigation. At 31 years of age he was too old for the front line. However, in the early hours of 2 August 1940, he was flying on a cross-country training exercise in a Fairey Battle aircraft and was killed when it crashed into a hill. Despite his untimely death, the legacy of his passion and enthusiasm for restoring old vehicles and aircraft to their former glory lives on at the Shuttleworth Collection.

Some of the most notable aircraft in the Collection are the five Edwardian aeroplanes, of which the 1909 Blackburn Monoplane is the oldest British aeroplane still in flying condition. What makes these old flying machines exceptional is that, weather permitting, they still fly. The oldest of all, with British civil registration G-AANG, is the Bleriot XI, still flying with the original engine, and also dates back to 1909 – just six years after the Wright brothers' aircraft first flew.

Restoration and maintenance work is carried out by full-time and volunteer engineers. The volunteers are all members of the 3,000-strong Shuttleworth Veteran Aeroplane Society (SVAS). These dedicated enthusiasts are crucial to the preservation and restoration of the Collection. In line with the founder's original intention, the Shuttleworth Collection puts an emphasis on restoring as many aircraft as possible to flying condition. There are typically about twelve airshows per year, including evening displays, which offer the opportunity to see aircraft that, in many cases, are the last of their type flying.

My connection with the collection started in 1979, while I was serving at the government research airfield at Thurleigh, known as RAE Bedford, only 18 miles north of Old Warden. I was introduced to the Collection's senior pilot, Dickie Martin,* by George Ellis, who was a classmate from the 1975 ETPS course.** George was also a test pilot at Bedford and was a volunteer pilot for the Shuttleworth Collection. The policy for selection as a pilot was that they should preferably be a qualified test pilot. This was aimed at ensuring that pilots had already proved themselves of above average ability – an entry condition for test pilot training – and adaptable at flying a variety of aircraft types with minimal training. This rationale could also be said to include other test flying attributes of acute safety awareness, teamwork and measured self-confidence.

---

* Richard 'Dickie' Martin, OBE, DFC, AFC (26 July 1918–1 September 2006) had served in the RAF during the Second World War and won a Distinguished Flying Cross and bar. After the war, he tested the early experimental jets that led to the development of the Hunter, Swift and Sea Vixen fighter aircraft. He left the RAF in 1953, with the rank of wing commander, to become a test pilot at the Gloster Aircraft Company, where he was later the chief test pilot and led development of the delta-wing Javelin fighter.

** See *Trials and Errors*, published by The History Press, 2015.

I was told at the outset not to expect to be flying during my first season. There was a philosophy of immersion in the practices surrounding historic aviation, as well as a subtle test of determination to continue despite spending a couple of hours helping to extricate aeroplanes from the hangars, push them out to the flight line and then reversing the whole procedure at the end of the display. From my point of view just being asked was a real thrill and being up close and personal, albeit on the ground, with these often unique flying machines was enough. Well, for the time being – the thought that I might get to fly them one day was sufficient motivation for me to keep turning up at the weekends.

In fact, in my second season I was asked if I would occasionally help out with the commentary from the top of the diminutive 'control tower' – another great honour and pleasure. Plus I did get some flying at Old Warden during 1980, with George Ellis in the Tiger Moth and solo in the DH.60G Cirrus Moth, as well as flying three visiting aircraft: Zlin Trener, Auster AOP.9 and Piper Cub. However, in 1981 I was unexpectedly posted from Bedford back to Boscombe Down, where I would be teaching trainee test pilots with ETPS. Due to a shortage of married quarters I was going to have to live on-base for the first year, so I told the senior pilot that I would like to take a year out while I was commuting weekly and only seeing my family at the weekends. I thought it a bit unfair on them for me to also be absent on many Saturdays and/or Sundays from April to October. Much understanding was shown and it was agreed that I could start again in 1982.

As it happened, my marriage broke up in 1982 and I became a single parent while holding down my job at ETPS. I couldn't spare the time so, very sadly, flying for the Shuttleworth Collection seemed to have fallen by the wayside. However, four years later I was posted to RAE Farnborough as OC Flying, an appointment that included the enviable task of flying the S.E.5a, which was then jointly 'owned and operated' by the Collection and the RAE. This meant that I had to reconnect with Old Warden and on 12 June 1987 I went there to meet John Lewis, who had taken over from Dickie Martin as chief pilot. We flew together in the Tiger Moth so that John could reassure himself that I was a fit person to be let loose in the S.E.5a. It was great to be back in an open-cockpit, 'taildragger' biplane and tackle all the challenges that come with an aeroplane of that era. I must have done enough to satisfy Mr Lewis because, after a light lunch, he walked me round the S.E.5 and helped me strap in and supervised the engine start. After that I was on my own!

However, being one of the two RAE S.E.5a pilots did not automatically confer me with access to the rest of the Collection's aircraft. I would still have to apply and do the 'apprenticeship' as before. But at least, after two seasons of displaying the S.E.5 under the joint RAE/Shuttleworth agreement, I became known at Old Warden again. When I had moved on from Farnborough, to Boscombe Down yet again, I reapplied to join the pilot list at Old Warden. Hence, on 2 May 1990 John Lewis and I once more committed aviation in the Tiger Moth. I passed that test as well and John sent me off to do twenty minutes' 'general handling' in the Tiger. I flew my first display in it at Old Warden on 16 May; I also displayed the Chipmunk that day – a familiar old chum!

I should impart just one more bit of background knowledge about that unique grass airfield in deepest Bedfordshire. There are a total of three grass runways for the use of Collection aircraft. The longest is aligned approximately south-east–north-west (130 degrees–290 degrees) and has a total length of about 2,250ft (685.8m), the second longest at about 1,700ft (520m) is orientated north-east–south-west (030 degrees–210 degrees). The third strip is much shorter, at about 700ft (213m), and is aligned between the other two (about 060 degrees–240 degrees); this is solely for the use of the lower speed collection aircraft that are especially susceptible to crosswinds. Visiting aircraft are only permitted to use 03/21.*

The arrangement of the runways allows a unique layout for the crowd line in that it is bent through 90 degrees opposite the intersection of the two main grass strips. This allows pilots to display aircraft in turns 'around the bend', which gives a great opportunity for views of the top surfaces for the onlookers and photographers. This feature exists at no other airshow venue that I know.

---

* Since I flew at Old Warden runway, 03/21 has been doubled in length but only for use during displays and mainly by the DH.88 Comet Racer.

8

Multiple Moths

DH HERMES MOTH

When I was flying for the Collection there were no less than seven aircraft at Old Warden with a name that included the word 'Moth'. However, one of them was owned by British Aerospace and lodged at the Collection; this was often flown and displayed by nominated BAe test pilots. One of the things one had to learn early on was which Moth was which – Cirrus Moth, Hermes Moth, Puss Moth, Hornet Moth, Tiger Moth etc., etc. Dickie Martin had a good way of doing it. I listened in to one of his briefings and heard: 'George – you fly the red one. David – you take the white one. Tony – you fly the big silver one, and I'll fly the blue one. Any questions? No – good, let's get on with it!'

The sobriquet 'Moth' was first used by de Havilland (DH) in the mid-1920s. Post-First World War, the company had been looking for an entry to the civil market and had tried two avenues.

The first was via a design built for the light aeroplane competitive trials sponsored by the *Daily Mail* newspaper; to be held in October 1923 at

Lympne, an airfield on the British south coast. The resulting diminutive, single-seat flying machine was the DH.53 Humming Bird. It was a monoplane with a 30ft wingspan, a loaded weight of 565lb and was initially powered by a 750cc (about 10hp) Douglas motorcycle engine. Despite its low power, DH chief test pilot Hubert Broad flew impressive aerobatic displays in it. Although the DH.53 did not win a prize, it did win orders from the Air Ministry. However, the aircraft's unreliable engines (various were tried) and limited flight envelope led to the eight ordered being put up for sale. The Shuttleworth Collection owns the first prototype, G-EBHX, and has tried manfully to keep it flying. Indeed, during my time with the collection it did fly occasionally but continued to suffer from engine problems. I never was invited to squeeze myself into its tiny cockpit; I can't say that I was disappointed!*

The other tack taken by DH was into the touring aircraft market. It designed an elegant-looking biplane with a double, tandem cockpit layout that could take the pilot (in the rear cockpit) and either one passenger and luggage or two passengers in the front. In the latter case a removable cover allowed room for the two passengers. This design was the DH.51 – it never received a name. The aircraft was larger than its contemporaries (such as the Blackburn B-2) with a wingspan of 37ft and a maximum weight of almost 2,500lb. The DH.51 first flew in July 1924. Although docile and pleasant to fly, its size was a disincentive for private owners; it meant hangarage and running costs would be more expensive than those for other, smaller tourers coming onto the market. Only three DH.51s were built. Once more, the Collection keeps the last of those three flying – more on it later.

So the upshot for Sir Geoffrey de Havilland and his team was to go down the small, two-seat biplane route and this led, in February 1925, to the first flight of a DH.60 Moth. The design started as a 30ft-span biplane with straight, square plan wings and two separate cockpits in tandem. In keeping with common practice, dictated by centre of gravity considerations, the rear cockpit was for the pilot and used for all solo flights. The original engine was a four-cylinder, in-line Cirrus engine that developed 60hp. Over the following three years, this engine was developed progressively so

---

* On 1 July 2012 the DH.53 crashed while being flown by Trevor Roche, who was then the chief pilot. Trevor was extricated from the cockpit and rushed to hospital, where tragically he died from his injuries. The cause of the accident was put down to a loss of control and not engine failure. Trevor was a very accomplished ex-RAF test pilot and Gulf War veteran.

that the 1928 Mark III version produced 90hp; and this motor was subsequently installed in all production DH.60 Cirrus Moths. All the engines in the DH.60 Moths were installed upright, so that the cylinder heads were on top. Another development also took place in that the undercarriage was changed from a straight axle to a split-axle design. This gave a much softer ride on rough ground and all Cirrus Moths were then designated DH.60X. This was the start of a long and illustrious line of light aircraft. It is arguable that the DH Moth, in all its guises, was one of the most successful light aircraft designs of all time. Now I'll describe in more detail some of the Shuttleworth Collection Moths and what they were like to fly.

DH.60X Hermes Moth – G-EBWD

G-EBWD is a very important aeroplane. It was built in 1928 and is the first aircraft that Richard Shuttleworth bought, which makes it the progenitor of the Collection. His landing in WD at the newly created Old Warden aerodrome in September 1932 marked the start of a remarkable career for this particular Moth. It now holds the world record for the aircraft that has been continuously operated for the longest time from a single location. Not long after acquiring WD, Richard re-engined it with a 105hp Hermes engine from the same stable as the Cirrus. While doing so he rerouted the long exhaust pipe from running down the left side of the fuselage to the right. That meant entering the cockpits from the left, where there was a narrow reinforced walkway on the wing, was much easier – especially when the engine had been recently run!

So let's go fly this unique flying machine. Walking around the outside, I check the condition of the fabric and the tension of the flying wires and, most importantly, that the wing-fold mechanism retaining pins are properly located and secure. The wings on many inter-war light aircraft could be folded back alongside the fuselage, allowing owners to store them in small buildings and even tow them to the nearest aerodrome or grass strip.

Now it's time to get aboard. The cockpit is quite small and entry is not helped by the lack of the fold-down flap added in later Moths. In fact, ingress to the front cockpit is very awkward because it is directly beneath the top wing and you have to climb through some of the bracing wires to get in. Thankfully, we fly it from the back seat. The only instruments in the front cockpit show airspeed and height, but there is a rather large, attractive, art deco clock!

In the rear cockpit the instrument panel (sometimes called the dashboard back in the day) is uncluttered and has only the essentials for safe, visual flight. There is an airspeed indicator (ASI), reading from 40 to 160mph; rpm and oil pressure gauges; a level flight bubble indicator and a contemporary altimeter. For directional information, an early model P-Type compass is mounted on the floor between the pilot's feet. Having checked the full and free movement of the throttle, and set it closed, the same full, free and correct check must be made of the flying controls. The rudder can be checked on this Moth because the tailskid is fixed to the fuselage and not the rudder; this may affect the ground handling later.* One thing that is very noticeable in this and other early Moths is the differential operation of the ailerons, of which there is one set on the lower wing. This helps reduce yaw generated by applying aileron, but I don't expect it to eliminate it!

Starting the engine, in common with the majority of light aircraft of the inter-war period, is effected by having a brave and friendly soul swing the prop. First, the fuel is selected on by turning a small lever in the pipe coming down from the 19-gallon tank in the upper wing centre section. The fuel tank contents are indicated by a float in a tube above the tank; not that easy to see, especially for a 'short-house' like me! Then, after a positive check that the magneto switches, located outside the cockpit on the fuselage between the cockpits, are off, the prop is turned over a few times to prime the carburettor. When everyone is ready, the throttle is cracked open half an inch and the front magneto switch is turned on.** Now is the time for the familiar call of 'Contact', at which point the man outside energetically swings the prop. If we've done everything correctly the engine will fire up with a few pops from the long exhaust pipe and is soon running at 800–900rpm. Now I switch on the other magneto switch and check that the oil pressure

---

* Tailskids were incorporated in aeroplanes from the very earliest days of aviation. Obviously a skid lifted the rear fuselage and tail surfaces clear of the ground. Tailskids could be fixed so that they did not move and simply absorbed the forces put on them by the aircraft on the ground. However, some were allowed to turn to make manoeuvring easier and the ultimate was to put the skid on the lower edge of the rudder. This gave the pilot direct control of direction on the ground. As hard runways started to replace grass, tailwheels replaced tailskids.

** Piston-engined aircraft are equipped with two spark plugs per cylinder, each supplied with high-tension current from separate magnetos. This gives redundancy as well as allowing the timing of the sparks to differ slightly to increase the efficiency and output of the engine. Hence there are two magneto switches.

is reading about 60psi; it will settle to about 40psi in flight. As WD is not fitted with a cylinder head temperature (CHT) gauge, a four-minute hold on the chocks follows for the engine to warm up. This pause is a good time to anticipate how the wind will affect getting out to the runway. I also turn each magneto switch off in turn, to make sure that the engine keeps going – this is called, rather macabrely, the 'dead-cut' check.

After the four minutes are up I make a wind-up signal to the man in white overalls outside; he breaks off from his own reverie and responds. Now is the time to check the correct operation of the magnetos. After holding the stick hard back and setting 1,600rpm, each magneto switch is turned off in turn. There should be a small drop in the rpm as each is switched; the rpm drop should not exceed 75. As it doesn't, I wave the chocks away and set off towards the runway in use. All the above starting procedure is common to most of the Collection's smaller aircraft with normal reciprocating engines. While some of the values of pressures and rpms may change, the basic routine stays the same; hence I will not repeat it in detail for similar types.

Now to employ a special technique for taxying fixed-skid aeroplanes with no brakes. To turn I must use a good boot-full of rudder carefully co-ordinated with a burst of power to generate slipstream over the rudder and effect the turn. The power bursts must be kept short, especially when going down-slope, or the speed may get too high and with no brakes it may all end in tears! This is why it is important to take into account the wind speed and direction as well as the condition of the grass. If in doubt get a couple of friendly white overalls to hold onto each wingtip and help to turn and brake the aeroplane for you.

Assuming that we've arrived in one piece at the holding point for the runway in use, I throttle back to 800–900rpm and quickly complete the simple pre-take-off checks. After a good visual check all around and a look at the diminutive 'control tower' to make sure that I'm receiving a green light, I open the throttle enough to roll forward and use the rudder to line up with the centreline of the strip. This is the time to see where the far end of the airfield intersects each side of the engine cowling up front; note it well because this is the three-point attitude we'll need when we land. Full throttle begets a throaty bark from the exhaust pipe and the little aircraft accelerates surprisingly well. The power to weight ratio with the Hermes engine gives WD a lively feeling. As I move the stick forward the tail comes up readily and as the ASI only starts reading at 40mph we are immediately ready to lift off the ground. Once airborne I hold a shallow climbing attitude until the speed arrives at 65 and then adjust it to hold 65–70mph in the climb.

If the day is fairly calm then the climb to a few thousand feet is a real pleasure. However, in common with most Moths, if it is turbulent then the ride can be much less comfortable. This is especially so with lateral disturbances, when lots of activity is required to keep the wings level with the rather inadequate ailerons.

At 3,000ft I level off and set cruise power of 1,900rpm; this will give us a speed of about 90mph and use about 8 gallons per hour, giving a still-air fuel consumption of about 11mpg. Now we're up here, let's check out the stalling characteristics. After a thorough visual check outside, all around and below, I pick a direction and roll out, closing the throttle as I do so. Holding the nose in the level flight attitude, the aircraft loses speed rapidly; all those wings and wires and fixed undercarriage add a lot of drag. As the speed falls below 40mph, WD definitely feels very loose and the ailerons become ineffective. But the rudder is still active and using my feet I can keep the sideslip to zero. The stick is fairly well back when the nose drops gently at a speed of probably 35–38mph; WD is now stalled. Recovery with forward stick and full throttle is prompt and once at 60mph I can safely climb back the 200–300ft that we've lost. It was all safe and predictable, as it should be for the average private pilot to deal with.

The Hermes Moth is moderately aerobatic and basic manoeuvres are permitted. The maximum allowed speed (VNE) is 124mph but 110 is sufficient for a loop or stall turn; a loop takes up about 500ft of sky. The early Moths don't give one confidence about rolling manoeuvres; the ailerons are a little heavy and the rate of roll at maximum deflection is poor. Barrel rolls are a better bet, but you need to get it rolling as soon as you get the nose high and use rudder to co-ordinate and help the roll rate. I make a note to myself that I won't be including aerobatics in my display.

On a calm summer's evening there is little to beat the aviation experience of puttering about in a DH Moth. The gentle whispering of the wind in the wires and the burbling engine up ahead doesn't disturb the unheard quiet of the pastoral patchwork drifting by below. Only the white chalk lines in the sky, tens of thousands of feet over our heads, speak of the modern era. Otherwise we could be on our way home from a visit to friends elsewhere, or just taking time out from the day-to-day realities of our 1930s' lives. It is amazing to think of all those brave and sometimes overambitious young flyers who took their DH Moths on journeys across the globe, blazing trails for those high-flying travellers to come.

But now it's time to head back and put this delightful little biplane back on the airfield from where it has operated for so many decades. With the throttle closed and holding a speed of 70mph, WD descends nicely, losing about 1,000ft per minute; the popping from the exhaust is now hushed and there's just the gentle breeze blowing around the cockpit. It's worth making a mental note of the attitude of the nose against the far horizon – this is the attitude to set quickly if the engine should ever stop. If we need to increase the rate of descent the best method will be to sideslip; this machine is of that era, before flaps and airbrakes, when sideslipping was a common technique. The rudder has plenty of authority to initiate and hold a good sideslip angle, but we must be aware that any roll generated will have to be controlled by the much weaker ailerons and we must lower the nose to keep the speed at a minimum of 70mph.

Now we have the airfield below, we turn downwind at 800ft, level off and set power for about 80mph to fly parallel with the runway. A quick check of the fuel and harness and we're set for landing. Abeam the beginning of the grass strip, we throttle back to just a trickle of power, let the speed come back to 75 and turn left towards the final approach path. Once lined up, we make a small adjustment to the attitude, use sufficient power to hold a 3–4 degree approach path angle and let the speed come back to 65mph. Once steadily descending towards the runway the speed can come back to 60 and, as we cross the threshold, raise the nose, check the speed is about 55 and make sure that the throttle is fully closed. Now for the classic three-point landing, we hold the aircraft airborne at 6in altitude, keep the stick coming back and watch the position of the nose until it reproduces the attitude we noted when we lined up for take-off. When the attitude gets there, we stop raising the nose and wait. If we've got the height right the little white Moth will drop gently onto the ground on all three 'points'. Very satisfying. If we land prematurely, just on the mainwheels, and overreact, the Moths will all bounce back into the air with alacrity. The redesigned undercarriage of the X models onward did reduce the ferocity of this embarrassing outcome.

Taxying back is a time to reflect on our impressions. The main one has to be that the controls are not classically well-balanced. The ailerons are a bit heavy for a light aircraft and the roll rate a bit sluggish. This is a marked contrast with the lightness and good response of the elevators and rudder. However, the delightful innate nature of this gem from the inter-war years overrides this drawback. There is a special pleasure to be had in flying a de Havilland Moth in the right weather conditions. G–EBWD is especially rewarding because Richard Shuttleworth gave it an additional 45hp over its predecessors; that's more than a 60 per cent increase in power, and that makes all the difference!

DH.60G Gipsy Moth – G-ABAG

The DH Moths' original Cirrus engines were built using some major parts from the French company Renault. In the late 1920s these parts became harder to get and hence more expensive. So Geoffrey de Havilland asked his chief designer, Frank Halford, to come up with a new but similar in-house engine. The result was the DH Gipsy 1, an in-line, four-cylinder, 5-litre engine that developed about 100hp. It was the genesis of a long line of engines that would power many aircraft in the years to come. The ultimate development of the Gipsy was a six-cylinder 200+hp engine; this was called the Gipsy Six or Gipsy Queen, depending on the exact application.

One of the first uses of the Gipsy was in the DH.60X Moth and de Havilland wanted to have a Gipsy Moth compete in the 1928 King's Cup Air Race – the most prestigious air race in the UK. Of the fourteen Moths that took part that year, three were Gipsy Moths, one of which won at a remarkable average speed of 105mph. To gain even more publicity and kudos, Geoffrey de Havilland flew a Gipsy Moth to an astounding altitude of 21,000ft and his chief test pilot, Hubert Broad, stayed airborne in one for twenty-four hours. That is a feat that I cannot begin to sympathise with – the discomfort and cold must have been almost unbearable. Those two really were 'Magnificent Men in their Flying Machines'!

Unsurprisingly, Gipsy Moths sold like hot cakes, many to overseas customers. Licensed production soon began in France, Australia and the USA. The Gipsy Moth was the aeroplane of choice for many attempts at very long-distance flights. Perhaps the most famous was that of Amy Johnson in G-AAAH, which she named *Jason* after the trademark of her father's fish business in Hull. Between 5 and 24 May 1930 she flew *Jason* 11,000 miles from Croydon Airport, just outside London, to Darwin in the Northern Territories of Australia. This amazing achievement meant that she became the first woman to fly solo from England to Australia.

She received instant worldwide recognition, the CBE from the King, and the Harmon Trophy.* Other long-distance Gipsy Moths were G-AAAK,

---

* The Harmon Trophy is a set of three international trophies, to be awarded annually to the world's outstanding aviator, aviatrix, and aeronaut (balloon or dirigible). The award was established in 1926 by Clifford B. Harmon, a wealthy balloonist and aviator. The awards are described by the Clifford B. Harmon Trust as: 'American awards for the most outstanding international achievements in the arts and/or science of aeronautics for the preceding year, with the art of flying receiving first consideration.'

flown by Francis Chichester from Australia to the tiny Norfolk and Lord Howe Islands in the South Pacific – an outstanding navigational feat* – and G-AAJP flown by John Grierson to various locations, including India, Russia and Iceland. The Gipsy Moth had come of age and was flown by hundreds of private and club pilots in the 1930s.

The Collection's Gipsy Moth was built in 1930 (Constructor's No. 1259) and registered as G-ABAG to the Bentley Motor Company; it is almost always referred to as the 'Bag Moth' by the Collection's pilots and engineers. AG had four different owners in the nine years leading up to 1939 and during that time the actor Ralph (later Sir Ralph) Richardson learned to fly in her. Having been stored during the Second World War, the aircraft was given to the Collection by the widow of its post-war owner, Douglas Hull. It flew its first public display on 28 August 1977.

The flying and handling characteristics of the 'Bag Moth' are very similar to those of the Hermes Moth. There was only a 5hp difference in motive power, so the performance was also very similar. The other two Cirrus Moths that I flew during my time with the Collection handled more or less the same, but their lower-powered engines meant that their overall performance was even less impressive! Also those earlier, lighter Moths were more restricted on maximum airspeed (91mph), aerobatics were forbidden and their approach and landing speed lower (55 reducing to 45mph). They were also much more susceptible to turbulence and wind. It was common for us to fly three Moths during one ten-minute display slot. This was mainly because we could do so little with them other than float around looking pretty, so having three up gave the crowd more to look at. We didn't necessarily try to fly them in formation but occasionally we would find ourselves occupying the same bit of sky!

DH.87b Hornet Moth – G-ADND

The DH.87 Hornet Moth was a 1934 design that sought to update the Moth series to a perceived requirement for more comfort and better performance of the earlier Moths. The first and very noticeable difference is

---

* In July 1967 Francis Chichester was knighted by Queen Elizabeth II for becoming the first person to sail single-handed around the world in nine months and one day. He named his ketch *Gipsy Moth IV*.

the enclosed cockpit with side-by-side seating. By the mid-1930s this was thought to be a selling point for its 'sociability', as well as protection from the wind and weather. Initially de Havilland's new biplane design had tapered wings. However, the rapid wing-drop that the pointed wingtips engendered at or near the stall was deemed to be unacceptable for the private owner at whom the Hornet Moth was aimed. DH replaced the tapered wings with more traditional, and safer, square-plan wings; this design became the DH.87b. The company even offered free replacement wings for any customers who had already purchased the original design! The Hornet Moth was sold in moderate numbers; 165 were built and some were exported and even assembled overseas.

The Shuttleworth Collection's Hornet Moth G-ADND was acquired in 1971 and its original 130hp Gipsy Major engine had been replaced with a 145hp version. Externally the aircraft was attractive and had a low-slung look to it, with a long exhaust pipe running under the fuselage beyond the wing trailing edge. Like other Moths, there were no flaps and a single pair of ailerons on the lower wings. The undercarriage was as per the X-Moth arrangement except that there was an additional strut coming out of the top of the engine cowling to each wheel axle. An unusual feature was that the fairing on this strut could be rotated to lie flat against the airflow, so acting as an airbrake; this odd feature was operated by a lever in the cockpit. I wasn't at all sure what effect it would have, so I would leave that till later!

The cockpit had doors on each side for entry. We flew it from the left seat, and the general layout was pretty conventional, except for the control column. This was a central one coming up from the cockpit floor but split into a Y shape, making a control stick grip available to each seat. Another 'new' feature on the Hornet Moth was the provision of brakes and a castoring tailwheel.

Starting was via a prop swing from a man outside, with all the normal drills before and after, but adding a check that the brakes were on. Once the magnetos had been checked then taxying was a straightforward business with judicious use of bursts of throttle and the castoring tailwheel helping to negotiate corners, and weaving to see clearly ahead. Having said that, the view ahead was better than the other Moths; the ground attitude seemed less nose-high and the engine was installed inverted.

On my first flight in the Hornet I got airborne easily as the 145hp and square, honest wings lifted us off the ground in about 250 yards. Once the speed was at 60kt, I throttled the engine back to 2,050rpm and climbed to 3,000ft so that I could fly around and get the feel of the aeroplane. I planned to stall it and do some stability and control checks. The climb performance turned out to be what I had expected and I was levelling off at 3,000ft about five minutes after take-off when something odd happened. As I throttled back to fly level at 80kt, a harsh vibration started.

Immediately I thought that it was an engine problem. But there was no indication of a malfunction with the Gipsy Major, the oil pressure was above 30psi and steady, and there were no signs of oil leaking outside. As the vibration was continuing even after I had throttled back a bit, I decided to take the aeroplane back and let the engineers look at it. I throttled right back to idle and let the speed come back to 60 and adopted a nose-down attitude to hold that speed. The vibration had reduced markedly with the reduction in rpm and airspeed. I was not far from the airfield so I made a left turn to glide downwind and make a descending circuit to land on the runway from which I had so recently departed. The Hornet's rate of descent was about 800ft per minute, so I was on finals only four minutes after the vibration had started. I remembered that this little Moth had airbrakes, so I located the operating lever on the left in case I needed to lose more height in order to make my touchdown point. In the event the 10kt headwind did the job for me and I touched down safely on the strip. I surprised myself with quite a passable landing. The nice handling in pitch really helped. I turned off the landing strip and shut down the engine.

It wasn't long before Andy Preslent, one of the Collection's aero engineers, had ambled over to find out what was going on. After I told him all about the incident, he did what I expected – he lifted the engine cowlings and peered inside at the still hot motor.

'Nothing obvious in here,' he said. 'We'll tow it up to the hangar and take a better look – check the plugs and that sort of stuff.'

Not long afterwards the chief engineer, Chris Morris, tapped me on the shoulder and said, 'We found out what was wrong with the Hornet Moth. Come and have a look.'

When we walked up to the pretty blue aeroplane, Chris pointed to one of the two propeller blades. 'See?' At first I wasn't sure what I was supposed to see. 'Compare it with the other one,' came the knowing advice.

Then it was obvious. The shiny brass strip fixed along two-thirds of the leading edge of one propeller blade wasn't there. The strip is there to stop erosion of the leading edge, especially in rain.

'That's what caused the vibration – when that came off, the prop went instantly out of balance,' said Chris. Well, that explained everything. The strip's departure coincided with me moving the throttle, hence my instant conclusion that it was an engine problem.

I did complete my conversion to the Hornet Moth later and displayed it several times. The only really remarkable thing about it was the asymmetric feel to the stick when applying aileron. Because of the offset from the pivot in the centre of the floor, instead of moving from side to side like a normal control column, it moved down to the left and up to the right. One soon got used to it, and this Moth was not much different to the others when it came to low roll power! Another oddity was that the 35-gallon fuel tank was behind the seats with the fuel cock and gauge on the forward face of the tank, between seats; however, the top of the tank made a very useful parcel shelf!

I also flew the Hornet Moth cross-country a couple of times, on errands for the Collection. With 2,050rpm set it cruised at 80kt and used about 8 gallons per hour. It was easy to trim and cruising at 2,000–3,000ft was very pleasant indeed, as well as being cost-effective. I did try the airbrake but it didn't appear to make a significant difference to anything!

DH.82A Tiger Moth G-ANKT (T6818)

The Tiger Moth is probably the DH Moth with which most people are familiar. It was developed as early as 1931, from the DH.80X Gipsy Moth, for use by the Elementary and Reserve Flying Schools as a military trainer. However, the schools were civilian organisations working under contract for the Air Ministry, so all the 'Tigers' flying during most of the 1930s were civilian registered. Military registration and camouflage colour schemes came with the outbreak of the Second World War. The main changes made to the Gipsy Moth were:

- General strengthening, including a plywood skin on the upper fuselage (instead of fabric).
- The replacement of the Gipsy III engine with the 130hp Gipsy Major, which was installed inverted to improve the view over the nose.
- Moving the centre section of the upper wing forward to allow easier egress from the front cockpit, especially if a parachute escape was

necessary. This, incidentally, gave the rather more attractive slight sweep-back to the upper wing.

The Collection's Tiger Moth was actually rebuilt from parts of three DH.82s purchased in the mid-1960s, in various states of disrepair. The most intact fuselage was that of G-ANKT, which had acquired the military registration of T6818. The rebuild was undertaken by two former Old Warden engineering apprentices and KT first flew as a Collection exhibit on 3 October 1977.

The Collection's Tiger Moth is the entry level aircraft for all Shuttleworth pilots. It has all the characteristics of an inter-war wings: open cockpit, strutted and wire-braced biplane, no brakes or flaps, and tailskid. However, the Tiger is a little easier to handle than some of the other Moths. Although still not endowed with powerful roll control, it does respond well to rudder and elevator inputs.

Aerobatics are allowed in the Tiger Moth so, after practice at a safe height, the basic manoeuvres of loops, barrel rolls, wingovers and stall turns can be flown during displays. As with most light aircraft of the era, one needs to keep a wary eye on the height if consecutive manoeuvres are flown as the general trend is downhill!

The Tiger Moth is a bit special for most pilots. However, when I first flew it, and that was before I had flown any other biplane, I was a little disappointed with its handling qualities. But that was probably because I had flown more than 1,200 hours in the Tiger Moth's replacement, DH Canada's Chipmunk, which had much better control harmonisation and handling qualities. In time I would compensate for the Tiger's shortcomings and I would display it regularly at Old Warden. Oddly enough, my final display in a Shuttleworth Collection aircraft would be in DH.82A Tiger Moth G-ANKT, not at Old Warden, but on the public days at the 1996 Farnborough International Airshow. A bizarre coming together of several strands of my flying career! I remember taxying off the grass strip in front of my old office in the control tower (now demolished) and being given a friendly wave by the pilot of the powerful late twentieth century Russian Sukhoi Su-27 fighter that was about to split the sky asunder for an appreciative audience. As the columnist Roger Bacon in *Flight International* magazine used to write … aaah de Havilland!

9

Bristol Boxkite and Avro Triplane

AVRO TRIPLANE IV

When I was flying with the Shuttleworth Collection there were no fewer than five Edwardian era* aeroplanes regularly flying in displays. They were:

Bleriot Type XI (1909)
Deperdussin (1910)
Bristol Boxkite (1910)*
Avro Triplane IV (1910)*
Blackburn Monoplane (1912)**

The Bristol Boxkite and the Avro Triplane were accurate replicas, but fitted with more powerful engines than the originals. They were built in 1964 for the highly successful film *Those Magnificent Men in their Flying Machines*.

---

* For this book I define the Edwardian era as 1901 to 1914.
** Some historians date the Blackburn from 1913 and the Triplane from 1911.

The Bleriot XI was the same model as the machine that Louis Bleriot used to make the first successful aerial crossing of the English Channel on 25 July 1909 and was acquired by Richard Shuttleworth in 1935. He also acquired the Deperdussin that same year and the aircraft was restored to make its first flight at Old Warden two years later. Both the Bleriot and the 'Dep' are only flown in near-calm conditions, performing straight hops; although I did once see the latter fly a circuit in the very capable hands of John Lewis. The Blackburn Monoplane was put into storage at the beginning of the First World War. It remained undiscovered until 1937, when Richard Shuttleworth bought it to add to his growing collection. However, it wasn't until 1949 that its restoration to flying condition was completed. The Collection's Blackburn is capable of flying circuits in calm conditions and is the oldest original British aircraft flying anywhere in the world.

Bristol Boxkite G-ASPP (BAPC2)

In August 1992 I was briefed for a conversion sortie in the Bristol Boxkite. However, on the evening that I was scheduled to fly it, after I had started the engine, there was a noticeable, but subtle, high-frequency vibration. After shutting down the engine, a small amount of damage was found on one blade of the wooden propeller. This had probably occurred during its previous sortie. It was decided that I could at least get used to moving around on the ground and fly it once the propeller was repaired. Moreover, quite a crowd had gathered to watch, having obviously delayed their departure after the day's display, so we didn't want to disappoint them! Sadly, another opportunity to commit aviation in this magnificent flying machine never arose before I left the Collection in 1996.

The Collection's Boxkite replica was built in 1964 by the F.G. Miles aircraft company at its Shoreham facility. Original plans for Henry Farman's Type III were used, as this was the basis of the Bristol-built version. The original 70hp Gnome rotary engine was replaced with a more modern 90hp Lycoming. After filming was finished, the aircraft was acquired by the Bristol Aeroplane Co. and then passed to the Shuttleworth Collection for preservation.

The pre-flight briefing had included a warning that the Boxkite was unstable in pitch and that I should be alert to changes in attitude and airspeed; not that the recommended speed range was large – between 30 and

45mph! The best method to avoid a pilot–induced oscillation (PIO) was going to be to watch the position of the foreplane against the horizon and use the attitude to control airspeed. The drag from the large wings and many wires and struts meant that most of the flight would be accomplished using almost maximum power. Small reductions in power and adjustment to the attitude would control speed and flight path.

The Boxkite has many unusual features, especially to a modern pilot, but perhaps the most bizarre is the way that the ailerons on all four wings hang down vertically when the aircraft is at rest. I was assured that they would be pushed up into the correct position once acted upon by the airflow and the appropriate set of slack wires underneath the aeroplane would tighten so that the ailerons could be operated in the usual way. I was told to make any turns with an initial bank angle of 10–15 degrees and balance the turn with the rudders – all three of them! They were located between the two tailplanes at the back end of the fragile-looking, uncovered rear 'fuselage'. Balance, that is zero sideslip, is achieved by keeping a piece of waxed string, attached to a bracing wire immediately below the forward elevator, pointing directly towards the pilot. In these old flying machines, with a marginal amount of thrust to overcome drag, any sideslip will increase the latter and *in extremis* could cause a descent into *terra firma*. Having used a similar string indicator in helicopters, I remembered that it works in the opposite sense to a slip ball instrument. This low-tech device is so important to safe flight and performance that the securing knot is checked before flight!

So to get aboard. Part of the briefing before flying the Boxkite is to make sure that one's trousers are tucked into one's socks. That's because there is no enclosed cockpit and one's feet stick straight out ahead into the airflow on the exposed rudder pedals! The result of open trouser legs could be inflation, like a Michelin man! The pilot's seat is fixed to a wooden platform on the lower mainplane, in front of the pusher engine. The pilot's seat is more than 6ft from the ground, with no safe way of climbing up to it. All is not lost as a helpful member of the support crew turns up with a ladder. This artefact actually looks about as old as the Boxkite! It is laid against the starboard inner wing leading edge and then it's just a case of climbing up carefully, fighting one's way through the forest of wires, and stepping across onto the platform on which the wicker seat is fixed. At this point the stick is in the way so it has to be pushed forwards so that the seat can be accessed. Once sitting down, with feet now on the rudder bar up ahead and the four-point harness attached, we can look around at what we have to work with.

There is little solid structure ahead – no engine cowling, no fuselage covering, just struts, wires and fresh air; an uneasy feeling of openness. Agoraphobia and/or vertigo beckon!

The next surprise is the length of the control column; the grip at the top is right in front of my face! One supposes that it needed to be that long to give sufficient leverage to operate the flying controls. Now a paradoxical problem arises; with all this open space the view ahead is the one thing that is obscured by one's own hand (or perhaps hands) and the forward elevator!

Next to start the engine. There is a very rudimentary collection of instruments mounted horizontally on a small wooden panel to the lower left of the pilot: airspeed indicator (ASI), oil pressure, cylinder head temperature (CHT) and rpm gauges. The two magneto switches are also there, as is a carburettor heat control and the throttle. Now for another new experience. Because the engine is behind the pilot, all the pre-start shouting has to be done over the shoulder. The fuel is switched on, the magnetos off and, using the accelerator pump in the Lycoming, the throttle is pumped a few times to prime the inlet manifold while the groundcrew turns the prop. Once all is ready, the throttle is cracked open half an inch and the 'Contact!' call is made. With the stick hard back and the right magneto on, the prop is swung. The engine start is announced by a loud clatter from the rear and the rpm and oil pressure increasing. After switching on the second magneto, checking that the oil pressure is good and setting 1,000rpm, there's a pause while the engine warms up to 105°C. When it does we can set 1,800rpm and check that both magnetos are working correctly, before we close the throttle and wave the chocks away.

I held the control column to the rear, increased power and we moved off in a very stately fashion. However, I now noticed that with the stick fully back the foreplane had rotated around its axis so much that I couldn't see very far ahead! Moving the stick back towards neutral soon fixed that problem. The ride over the grass was surprisingly soft, much better than many of the other aircraft at Old Warden. That multi-wheeled, bungee-sprung undercarriage worked well! I experimented with turning and found that quite good control could be achieved by using full rudder in the desired direction and short bursts of power. It then struck me that part of the feeling of sedate progress was because there was no slipstream from the engine. I trundled around for a few minutes, wishing fervently that I could just open the throttle to max and float off into the evening sunset. But it wasn't to be and, in the end, this was as near to becoming a Boxkite pilot as I would ever get.

Of course, before I even got this far I had seen this magnificent and rather strange-looking flying machine take to the evening air. I had also talked to those who had successfully flown it. The overall opinion was that while the lack of longitudinal stability was a challenge, being able to safely fly more than a straight 'hop' and actually make majestic progress around the airfield at a respectable altitude was a reward worth the effort and concentration.

Avro Triplane IV G-ARSG (BAPC1)

However, I did fly an Edwardian flying machine, albeit another faithful replica: the Avro Triplane IV. Alliott Verdon Roe was a British aviation pioneer who designed and flew his own flying machines. Quite early in his experiments he decided that three narrow chord (or high aspect ratio) wings were better than two broad ones and would give more lift for less drag. He designed and flew three variations on this theme before arriving at the Triplane IV. None of these machines were put into series production but the lessons he learned led to two very successful biplanes: the Avro 504 and the later Avro Tutor, both of which became trainers for the RAF, operating well into the 1930s. The Collection's Avro Triplane was built by the Hampshire Aero Club at Eastleigh, near Southampton, in 1964 for the aforementioned magnificent film. There is one surviving, original Avro Triplane in the Science Museum, but the Shuttleworth airframe was thought to be of sufficient technical interest to warrant preservation in flying condition and was acquired for the Collection when filming had finished.

My conversion to the Triplane was, like that for the Boxkite, scheduled for the evening following the 27 June 1992 afternoon display at Old Warden. As was usual, I had spoken to a couple of pilots who had flown the aeroplane before; one of them being George Ellis. He waxed lyrical about this essentially 70-year-old flying machine. But there were words of caution – mainly about the very poor lateral control conferred by the wing warping system, in lieu of ailerons. I had made notes of speeds and other numbers and walked out to the rather flimsy-looking machine with a mixture of eager anticipation and awareness of the responsibility that comes from getting airborne in the world's only flying Avro Triplane.

A walk round the aircraft to make sure that the fabric looked undamaged and the myriad wires all seemed to be connected also reinforced some of the thoughts I had about how it might fly. There was no covering on the triangular section fuselage aft of the 'cockpit' and there was no fin at the end; just a rudder – which looked a bit too small. So I couldn't expect much in the way of directional stability. It was all going to be down to me using the little rudder. At the front end the engine was unadorned with tappet covers or any form of cowling; I could expect to receive a mist of oil swept back in the slipstream. Goggles on from start-up to shut down! The engine stuck up in line with the pilot and the small cylindrical fuel tank was suspended from the top wing. It looked like the view directly ahead would be minimal! Finally, how on earth do I get into the cockpit?

Well, that problem was overcome with the Collection's venerable wooden ladder. Once up there, having negotiated a way through the wires, I sat down. Although my feet were inside the narrow, enclosed hole in front of me, I was sitting more on the fuselage than in it. I looked behind me before I strapped in; I could see clear down to the ground and the empennage seemed as though it might follow me more out of a sense of curiosity than conviction. I resolved not to repeat this exercise in the air! In front of me was a great view of the back of the Hermes engine and, above that, the fuel tank. Not only that but the upper and middle wings restricted the upward and downward views as well. Closer to me was the rudimentary 'instrument panel'. It was furnished with an ASI and altimeter (although I wasn't sure why!) and an oil pressure gauge, as well as the magneto switches and placard from the CAA that illogically announced 'no smoking' and 'no aerobatic manoeuvres'! It took me a while to locate the rpm gauge – it was mounted on the rear of the engine block in what seemed like the middle distance. Getting aboard had not only been hampered by the nest of wires outside but also by the unusual set of flying controls in the cockpit. The most noticeable was a leather-covered steering wheel that was mounted on a bar that went through the rim of the cockpit to two plates that were connected to the elevators by wires. So fore and aft movement of the wheel controlled pitch and rotary movement warped the wings to roll the aeroplane. I tried both to make sure that they worked correctly. Rotation of the wheel did make the wingtips of the top and middle wings move, but it was not easy and considerable rotation and force was needed to effect much change. Finally I tried moving the rudder. Because of the triangular section of the fuselage, the distance between the two small blocks of wood that moved the rudder was tiny and made me feel that I should have, like an F1 racing driver, worn light trainers!

I was now as ready as I was going to be, so I called out that the fuel was on, the throttle was closed and the magneto switches were off. At this a man appeared on the right-hand side of the engine and stuffed a rag dripping with fuel into the inlet manifold. Another man turned the prop over. When they were satisfied that the engine was sufficiently primed, I got a thumbs up. Goggles down, throttle set, switches on, 'Contact!' The engine burst into life and I checked that the oil pressure had risen, set 800rpm and then had to wait four minutes before carrying out the run-up to 1,600rpm to check the magnetos. In the meantime I found myself intrigued by the sight of the exposed rocker arms up front moving rapidly up and down. I could feel and smell the oily mist being freely distributed by the motor.

Once the mag drops had been checked satisfactorily, I throttled back and waved the chocks away. As it happened, on that calm summer's evening I didn't have far to taxi to the south-easterly runway. Steering the Triplane the short distance was not too hard and the ride on the four sprung wheels was soft. Once lined up on the runway, I opened the throttle fully and we set off at a leisurely pace. It was easy to keep straight and at about 35mph the machine lifted off sedately. I held the attitude until 45mph was showing on the ASI. We were actually climbing at a steady, if not astonishing rate, so I decided to try to make sure that we were going straight. I had been told that when there was zero sideslip then the warm air from the exhaust stubs on the left side of the engine should be felt on the left side of my face and that cold, damp air from the inlet manifold should be felt on the right side. I cautiously moved the tiny rudder pedals to check out if this advice was valid. It was! As I passed a couple of hundred feet I noticed that the cars leaving the airfield were overtaking me.

Just as I pondered whether to try the wing warping, I hit a burble of turbulence and the left wing dropped quite sharply by about 10 degrees. Adrenalin peaked and I wound the wheel with my right hand, the left still holding the throttle fully open. Now I remembered why I had tightened the throttle friction nut. It was time to use both hands on the wheel. The left wing had now reached about 15 degrees, so I wound the wheel hard to the right. The wings lazily came back to level. I did not use rudder because I had been told that this would not enhance the roll rate and only generate more undesirable slip. I kept going straight ahead and levelled off at 500ft, throttling back just a little to hold 45mph; the maximum allowed was only 50!

Now was the time to turn – anyway I had to unless I was going to land elsewhere! In the earliest days of fixed-wing aviation the notion was that directional control would be like that of a boat; hence the use of the word 'rudder' for the vertical, movable bit at the back end. Because using the rudder alone might cause the wings to depart from horizontal flight, ailerons or wing-warping was built in to allow the pilot to keep the wings level. However, those very early pioneers soon discovered that applying a boot-full of rudder and trying to hold the wings level was not only very uncomfortable, but caused lots of drag, losing critical amounts of speed and leading to loss of control or height – or both! In the end the early teaching was to lead with lateral control but balance with rudder. With the very low speeds of those early flying machines the rates of turn at low bank angles were more than adequate for the job of turning corners.

So, taking a good breath, I applied a hefty turn to the wheel and used the rudder to keep the warm dry/cold wet airflow on the correct sides of my face. I stopped at 15 degrees of bank and held the altitude at 500ft. The Triplane went round nicely. Because of the low roll rate, I made sure that I started to roll out well ahead of the direction that I wanted to go in. I was now headed back over the airfield. It was frustrating that my view dead ahead was so restricted as I knew that there were still some visiting aircraft to depart; I just had to hope that I was flying something that looked so strange that it would grab their attention! I was now relaxing a bit more and actually enjoying this unique experience. I wanted to discover the attitude I would need if the engine quit. So I reapplied full power and climbed to 800ft. During the couple of minutes that this took I wiped my goggles and refreshed myself on the recommended gliding speed: 45mph. I levelled off and turned once more so that I was headed back over the airfield. I gave myself a mental countdown '3, 2, 1, Now!' closed the throttle and pushed the nose down. The speed dropped rapidly at first but then it recovered to 45. The nose was lower than I had expected and I guessed that the rate of descent was about 800ft per minute. Having noted that final attitude it was time to go back.

By now I had come to an arrangement with the Triplane – I would handle it carefully if it didn't frighten me! A couple more cautious descending turns brought me to a final approach position at 300ft with the speed at 45mph. Even descending at about 300ft per minute, I still had a good amount of power on and I resolved to treat this a bit like a Buccaneer approach and landing – don't throttle back fully until the wheels are on the ground. I'd been told that the landing was the easiest bit so I was not quite as much on edge as I had been heretofore! It all went to plan. I didn't worry too much about the touchdown point and just held a steady descent at 40mph until I was just above the ground, I made the smallest of attitude changes and the lovely little veteran just sat down perfectly on three points. I closed the throttle and she stopped dead. Amazing!

Two gallant young men came towards me as I turned off the runway and walked the wingtips back to my parking place. As we trundled gently across the grass I tipped my proverbial hat at those pioneers of the beginning of the twentieth century. I had flown this 1910-designed flying machine using 70hp more power than Alliott Verdon Roe had back then. I know that ignorance can be bliss, but it still required men of courage and vision to break into the new science and art of aviation. Gentlemen, I salute you!

10

First World War

SE 5a

In the 1980s and early '90s, the Shuttleworth Collection had six aeroplanes from the 1914–18 period. They all flew and were:

Avro 504K – Trainer
Sopwith Pup – Single-seat fighter
Sopwith Triplane - Single-seat fighter
Bristol F.2b - Two-seat fighter and light bomber
Royal Aircraft Factory S.E.5a - Single-seat fighter
Luft-Verkehrs-Gesellschaft (LVG) C.V1 – Two-seat observation and
    light bomber

At the time of writing the LVG is no longer with the Collection. However, a Bristol M.1c and a Sopwith Camel, both replica single-seat fighters, have been added; the rest remain as flying examples of their types. I flew the S.E.5a and the Bristol Fighter.

S.E.5a G-EBIA (F904)

In late 1986, when I took up the appointment of OC Flying at RAE Farnborough, I was delighted to find that one of my many duties was to fly the S.E.5a that was then jointly owned and operated by RAE Farnborough and the Shuttleworth Collection. I first flew this restored, original, First World War fighter on Friday, 12 June 1987 at Old Warden, after a check flight with John Lewis in the Collection's Tiger Moth. I have previously described the aircraft, its history and flying it in my book *More Testing Times*, but for those who have yet to discover that tome I will reproduce most of the text here.

First, the history and background to the S.E.5a. In 1916 Farnborough's Royal Aircraft Factory* design team of Henry Folland, John Kenworthy and the chief test pilot, Major Frank Goodden, were working on a new fighter. They called it the Scout Experimental Number 5 – S.E.5 – and it was built around a newly available 150hp Hispano-Suiza 8,V8 water-cooled engine. The S.E.5 was designed to be a stable gun platform that should be easier to fly and outperform the rotary-engined fighters already in service; aircraft such as the Sopwith Camel. The first of three S.E.5 prototypes flew on 22 November 1916. The original two prototypes were lost in crashes due to a weakness in their wing design. One of these accidents, on 28 January 1917, killed Frank Goodden. The third prototype underwent modification before production commenced. Like the other significant Royal Aircraft Factory aircraft of the First World War, the S.E.5 was inherently stable, making it an excellent but manoeuvrable gun platform. It was one of the fastest aircraft of the war. While the S.E.5 was not as agile in a fight as the Sopwith Camel, it was much easier and safer to fly, particularly for novice pilots. The S.E.5 had one synchronised 0.303in Vickers machine gun to the Camel's two, but it also had a wing-mounted Lewis gun. That was on a Foster mounting, which gave the pilot the option to fire at an enemy aircraft from below, as well as providing two guns firing forward. The mounting also allowed the pilot to lower the gun so that he could change the magazine drum in flight; spare magazines were carried in the cockpit.

Only seventy-seven S.E.5 aircraft were built before production moved to the improved S.E.5a, which differed from the S.E.5 in the type of engine

---

*   With the formation of the Royal Air Force on 1 April 1918 the 'Factory' was renamed the Royal Aircraft Establishment.

installed: a geared 200hp Hispano-Suiza 8b, turning a large, four-bladed propeller. However, the troublesome, geared 8b engine was prone to serious reduction gearbox problems. Sometimes the propeller and even the entire gearbox separated from the engine in flight. The introduction of the 200hp Wolsey Viper, a high-compression, direct-drive version of the Hispano-Suiza 8, solved the S.E.5a's engine problems and was adopted as the standard powerplant. In total 5,265 S.E.5s, the vast majority S.E.5as, were built by six manufacturers.

The S.E.5 entered service with the Royal Flying Corps (RFC) in March 1917. The first S.E.5 squadron did not fly its first patrol until 22 April 1917 and pilots quickly came to appreciate its strength and fine flying qualities. However, at the outset it was held to be underpowered until the more powerful S.E.5a began to replace it in June 1917. Some sixteen squadrons equipped with the S.E.5a remained in RAF service for about a year after the war. A number of these machines found civilian roles and became popular for racing and skywriting.

Fast forward to 1955 and cue the appearance of RAF test pilot Air Commodore Allen Wheeler CBE.* While visiting the Armstrong-Whitworth company's flight shed at Whitley, near Coventry, he spotted a rather dilapidated S.E.5a hanging from the roof. It had last been used by a skywriting and barnstorming company and had the civil registration G-EBIA. Newly retired Air Commodore Wheeler, who was a trustee of the Shuttleworth Collection and one of their pilots, spotted this potential trophy to add to the Collection. Using his renowned powers of persuasion, he acquired the S.E.5a and had it transported to RAE Farnborough, where it was restored over a period of almost four years by engineering staff and apprentices. The aircraft was finished in the RFC colour scheme of the day and re-allocated its original military registration of F904. It flew for the first time after this restoration in August 1959, equipped with a Hispano engine. An agreement was struck between the RAE and the Shuttleworth Collection that the S.E.5a should be a shared asset, primarily housed, exhibited and flown at Old Warden, but transferred to Farnborough during the summer to be displayed at venues in southern and western England. During the latter detachments the aircraft would be serviced and supported by Farnborough personnel and flown by the two most senior RAE test pilots.

---

* Between 1941 and 1943 Allen Wheeler commanded the Performance Testing Squadron at Boscombe Down and, later, the Experimental Flying Department at RAE Farnborough.

In 1975 the CO at Farnborough, Group Captain 'Polly' Parrat, suffered a catastrophic engine failure and had to carry out a forced landing in a field. Despite his best efforts the aircraft was damaged and the undercarriage had to be partly rebuilt. A Wolsey Viper engine was found and the decision was made to install it, so bringing the S.E.5a back up to its full specification.

My first encounter with this diminutive biplane had been at Farnborough in 1976 when I watched the CO of the day, Gp Capt Reggie Spiers, fly it from the grass not far from the HQ of the Experimental Flying Squadron, where I was employed as a test pilot. It was a magical sight to see and hear a real First World War fighter, not a replica, soar into the late afternoon sky over the airfield from where the type had originated sixty years earlier. A sight and sound that would stay with me for a long time. That was the first of several such flights I watched, as the OC Flying, Wing Commander David Bywater, also flew the S.E.5 as part of his duties.

In 1986, as OC Flying, it was my turn. The aforementioned twenty-minute check flight in the Tiger Moth seemed to have satisfied John Lewis that I was a fit person to be allowed to fly the S.E.5a. After a guided tour of the tiny cockpit and wise words on what to watch out for, John gave me an aide-memoire to put in my kneepad. As we strolled towards the purposeful-looking fighter, the two groundcrew were ready and waiting. We walked round the S.E.5 to check that all was well visually. John showed me how to check the tensions of the flying wires and then it was time to climb aboard. This was achieved by poking my left foot into the recessed step on the lower longeron of the port side of the fuselage and then athletically swinging my right leg into the cockpit. During this manoeuvre it is vital to keep a weather eye on the butt of the Lewis gun jutting out behind the upper wing. It was neatly positioned to give a nasty bump to the head of a careless pilot! Once sat down, the cockpit fitted snugly around my upper arms. Four canvas seat straps secured me in place and I checked that the two sets of ignition switches were off and that the throttle moved fully and freely before it was closed.

The instrument panel is, with a couple of exceptions, definitely of its time. The original pattern, large airspeed indicator (ASI), centrally located compass and aneroid barometer pretending to be an altimeter are the flight instruments that remind you of the aircraft's age. To go along with these are the rpm indicator, coolant temperature and oil pressure gauges, and fuel tank contents indicator, as well as petrol and air selectors, all let into a varnished wooden panel. Below the compass is a 'level indicator', consisting of a bubble in a curved tube. This was the only pilot aid for flying in cloud, which, thankfully, we were not permitted to do! There are also various plates with instructions on them. Some of these are there at the insistence of our modern aviation regulators – the most unhelpful of which is one stating 'no smoking'! To enhance the vintage dials are a few modern instruments, situated high and on the right of centre, under the coaming: among them a more accurate ASI and altimeter. So as not to upset the purists who might want to look into or even photograph the cockpit in the museum, these modern interlopers can be covered with a matching wooden panel!* At the top left is the breech of the Vickers machine gun; it must have been very noisy when it was being used.

In my preparations to get things moving I also made sure that the shiny lever on the left that operated the 'Venetian blind' radiator shutters in the S.E.5's nose moved freely and then set it closed. The most complex part of the S.E.5 cockpit is the fuel system, which has two rotary selector knobs, one for selecting the source and destination for the fuel and one for the source of the air pressure that impels the fuel to the carburettors. There is also a rather unattractive arrangement of brass pipes on the lower part of the instrument panel and a hand-pump down by my left leg; that was there for emergency fuel tank pressurisation should the engine-driven pump fail. As a last resort there is a small reserve fuel tank in the centre section of the wing; this contains 4 gallons and should give a maximum of twenty minutes' flying time.

I checked the full and free movement of those flying controls operated by the stick, which is topped with a spade grip, bound with string, and has in its centre two thumb-operated firing levers, one for each gun. As the tailskid was fitted to the bottom of the rudder, checking rudder travel would have to wait until we were on the move. The S.E.5a is fitted with an innovative longitudinal trimming system for its time – a variable incidence tailplane. This was operated by a notched wheel down by my left thigh; I had checked it earlier and set the recommended seven divisions nose down.

I then used the pump by my left knee to get the air pressure in the fuel system up to 2.5psi. The strokes on the pump had to be made at just the right rate otherwise a very rude noise would emanate from the pressure relief valve. I didn't want anything blowing 'raspberries' today! The final action was to give a few strokes on the Kigass priming pump, after which the man out front turned the prop to draw the fuel into the inlet manifold.

---

* My sources tell me that these modern instruments have now been removed.

When that was finished he took up his position ready to swing the propeller and called that he was all set. I moved the throttle forward about half an inch and switched the rather unusual brass rotary magneto switch on the port cockpit wall to '2' and the starter magneto switch to 'on'.** 'Contact!'

The brave soul out front gave the prop a good heave and stepped aside. The starter magneto handle protruded from the right side of the cockpit and the man with the easier job wound that frantically just after the prop had started to move. With a pop and a crack the engine burst into life; I immediately caught it with the throttle, checked that the oil pressure had risen and set about 1,000rpm to help the now throbbing Viper to warm up. Then I switched the starter magneto to 'off' and the normal magneto to '1+2'. While waiting for the radiator coolant temperature to rise above 60°C, when I could increase the engine rpm, I checked that the magnetos were both working correctly by turning the switch to 1 and then 2 to make sure that the engine kept running.

As soon as I saw that the temperature had risen sufficiently, I stuck my left arm out into the slipstream and gave a rotating, wind-up signal. Then a couple of burly bystanders laid themselves across the rear fuselage to stop the tail rising, which can happen with some of the more powerful aircraft. When I was given a thumbs up from out front I wound the engine up to 1,500rpm, and checked that the oil pressure was what it should be. I turned off each magneto in turn to check that the drop in rpm didn't exceed about 100rpm and that it recovered when I turned each back on. It was time to go. With the throttle closed I waved the chocks away and set off across the grass towards the runway threshold.

On the ground I found the S.E.5a quite easy to manoeuvre; I just had to remember that there were no brakes. The knife-like tailskid moved with the rudder and dug into the ground, so turns were easy to make, especially if I used a simultaneous, judicious and brief burst of power. The blunt, high nose meant that I had to exercise the steering by weaving along so that I could clear the area ahead of me and not bump into anyone. I also made a mental note of where the near horizon intersected the nose; this would be the three-point attitude that I would try to achieve just before landing.

** The starter magneto is an additional device that gives a larger and correctly timed spark when starting engines of early piston-engined aeroplanes. It was operated by a rotary handle, usually in the cockpit or occasionally outside for operation by groundcrew.

Once at the holding point I completed the brief pre-take-off checks. Perhaps the most important of these vital actions was to make sure that the fuel was coming from the 28-gallon main tank (quaintly called the 'service' tank), and not the little reserve one up in the wing. The coolant temperature was also worth checking. If it was getting near 80°C, then opening the radiator shutters was a really good idea, especially on a summer's day when going straight into a display. The reason for this is twofold. First, it's not good for the health of the engine if it gets too hot. Second, the coolant header tank is alongside the reserve fuel tank in the wing root above and ahead of the cockpit. If the engine gets too hot the expansion of the now very hot liquid in the header tank encourages it to flow out through the overflow pipe, which terminates at the inboard wing trailing edge, not far from my head. In flight the hot water flows away in the slipstream, but after landing it drips into the prop wash and gets blown onto the driver's visage; ouch! 'Keep your goggles on after landing,' was a good bit of advice.

The same thing could happen with the reserve fuel tank, especially while taxying in, when the fuel could start to siphon out of its overflow pipe on the port side. Sometimes, after parking, there was a regular, intermittent hissing noise, coupled with small puffs of white smoke coming off the hot exhaust pipe right next to the cockpit. The temptation to stand up quickly and leap over the side was tempered by the presence of the Lewis gun butt directly above one's head. Eventually this pipe was rerouted outboard so that it dripped onto the grass and not the hot exhaust pipe.

The take-off, especially directly into wind, was relatively easy and the aircraft accelerated well. The rudder was very effective for keeping straight and the tail came up readily with just a light forward pressure on the stick. After lift-off, at about 50mph, I accelerated to 60 and climbed on full power, delighting in the fact that I was flying a bit of history; this fighter was already 27 years old when I was born! I climbed to 3,000ft over Old Warden and set up for a straight stall. As with all biplanes, especially those with flat noses, the S.E.5 slowed down rapidly when the throttle was closed. I tried to keep the deceleration to about 1–2mph per second by descending slowly, so that I could get a good feel for the way the aircraft responded to gentle control inputs. As I had been briefed, the effect of applying aileron at less than 45-46mph was about zero: despite having four ailerons the aircraft didn't roll at all. Rudder had been effective at rolling it until then, but I didn't want to be applying rudder near the stall – spinning was not allowed, nor was it sensible at this height! The stall happened in a conventional way at 42–43mph, after a noticeable buffeting the nose dropped despite my efforts to keep it on the horizon. There was no tendency to roll.

Recovery with forward stick, full power and rudder to stop any yaw was immediate and very effective; we lost about 200ft. *Note to self: never fly below 50mph, except near the ground when landing.* Also: *Always land into wind.* Kicking off drift with rudder just before touchdown will beget roll and the ailerons won't stop that happening. Result – probably dinging a wingtip or worse.

I flew some steep turns and wingovers, then accelerated to the maximum allowed speed of 150mph, which needed quite a steep dive and made a lot of noise and buffeting round my head! Time for a loop from 130mph and then a stall turn; they worked fine.* After that I practised an engine failure and was astounded how quickly and how far I had to push the nose down to keep the recommended gliding speed of 60mph.

Now it was time to go back and try to land this little beast. I flew into the circuit and set up for a downwind leg at 1,000ft and 70–80mph. After checking all the usual things and setting full nose-up trim (which would help during the landing), I turned towards the final approach at 70mph, then lined up with the runway at about 200ft and let the speed decline slowly from 60 to 50mph as I crossed the hedge. As I flew over the beginning of the grass runway I closed the throttle and slowly raised the nose to the three-point attitude that I had memorised from taxying out. I held it there as the nice little fighter settled sweetly onto the ground. *I hope John was watching that one,* I thought. However, I throttled up to try another full circuit; perhaps pushing my luck! The second circuit and landing were fine; it just showed how well designed the S.E.5 had been from the outset. I taxied back to the parking spot with a big grin. When I dismounted, trying to avoid the hot exhaust pipe en route to the ground, John had one of his own for me. What a wonderful day!

Over the next two years I would fly the S.E.5a many more times, with displays at various locations, including RAF Odiham, RAF Abingdon and RAE Bedford, as well as flying several transits between Farnborough and Old Warden. It was during the first of these that I decided to test just how stable the S.E.5a was. I was flying straight and level at 2,000ft and 90mph.

---

* About five years later the CAA reviewed all the Shuttleworth aircraft permits and stopped most of them from carrying out aerobatics. This led to yet more plaques in cockpits; the most ridiculous of which was the one declaring 'no aerobatic manoeuvres' in the 1910 Avro Triplane!

Having trimmed the aircraft to maintain level flight, I took my hands off the stick. I kept my feet on the rudder pedals so that I could use that to correct any lateral upsets and even turn the aircraft through small heading changes. After twenty minutes the little warplane had not deviated from the height and speed one iota; well done, Mr Folland et al.!

When I rejoined the Collection in May 1992 I had to wait just over a year before I could re-qualify on the S.E.5a and it became a regular entry in my logbook. I only had two airborne problems in it. The first was when I was part of an 'aerial battle' display, with the Bristol Fighter, the Sopwith Pup and the German LVG. I climbed to position overhead awaiting the other Brits to follow and then we were going to pounce on the low-flying LVG. But as I throttled back to level off, the engine started misfiring badly. I thought that it might have been magneto trouble and decided to get back on the ground ASAP.

Because we didn't fly with radios, all I could do was shut the throttle and turn back towards the airfield. That was my first mistake! I tried to turn before I had lowered the nose sufficiently to gain the gliding speed of 60mph. The S.E.5 rewarded me by refusing to bank – and then I remembered; the ailerons don't work below 45mph! I stopped trying to roll and pushed the nose down, got to 60mph and then tried again – it now rolled nicely into the turn. Of course, the other three members of our little pageant couldn't work out what I was doing, but they got out of the way and I touched down safely, turned off the landing strip and shut down. It was a magneto problem and the engineers fixed it before the next display day.

The other time that the fine little fighter let me down (literally) was after I had participated in a historical flypast of several Shuttleworth aircraft at the 1995 International Air Tattoo at Fairford in Gloucestershire. On the way back to Old Warden, on a delightful summer's Sunday afternoon, I noticed that the fuel tank air pressure had dropped. When it got below the safe minimum I changed the air input from the engine-driven pump to the hand pump and started pumping myself. After a while even this did not seem to be working and I was still too far from Old Warden to use the twenty minutes' worth of gravity-fed petrol in the reserve tank.

We had fitted a very rudimentary VHF radio set for the transit so I thought that I had better let someone know that I needed to land soon. I was about halfway between RAF Brize Norton and Oxford Kidlington Airport so I selected the Brize Approach frequency and made a 'Pan' emergency call. I selected the reserve tank and headed for Kidlington, which had a large grass area that would be safe for landing on. I heard nothing on the radio so I tried again. Then I heard a reply, but it was unreadable. I told the controller that I would be landing at Kidlington and asked him to telephone them.

There was a big area of grass east of the main runway and I flew over it to select a landing direction into what wind there was. There were no visible obstructions so I made my approach and landed safely. Being a Sunday, there seemed to be little other activity. After parking near the taxiway I shut down and climbed out. My arrival had apparently gone totally unnoticed! I walked over towards a building and was greeted by a young man who had finally spotted that there was a First World War fighter sitting on the airfield. It transpired that no phone call had been received from Brize Norton, but that didn't affect the hospitality that I was shown.

After several telephone calls to Old Warden I was told that someone would arrive 'later' to try to fix the aircraft. In fact, only a couple of hours passed before my old friend John Stoddart, the Collection's S.E.5 specialist engineer, turned up with his trusty tool kit. He dismantled the pump, discovered that the diaphragm was totally useless and replaced it. He helped me start up and the air and fuel pressures leapt eagerly to normal readings. A grin and a thumbs up to John were sufficient to signal that all was well. Within an hour I was back at Old Warden, pushing the S.E.5 back into the hangar.

My displays in the S.E.5a, before the CAA banned aerobatics, included stall turns, loops and wingovers with plenty of low flypasts for the photographers, especially 'round the corner' at Old Warden. I was allowed by my display authorisation to fly as low as 100ft on straight flypasts and not below 300ft during the recovery from aerobatics. I never tried to roll the S.E.5 through a full 360 degrees, although a high pull-up and half roll was feasible as a turnaround manoeuvre. The S.E.5a was a delight to display.

Out of the 130-plus aircraft types that I have flown the S.E.5a is one of my firm favourites, where it stands along with the Spitfire and the Lightning high on the list of all-time great fighters. I have given talks on the merits, and drawbacks, of those three warplanes and what they were like to fly. An interesting thought that I share with my audience is that there was just forty years separating the first flights of the S.E.5 and the Lightning, with the Spitfire sitting neatly in the middle.

Bristol F.2b G-AEPH (D8096)

The Bristol Fighter first entered service with the RFC on the Western Front in March 1917. It was armed with a fixed, forward-firing, synchronised 0.303in Vickers machine gun and a Lewis gun mounted on a Scarff ring in the rear gunner/observer's cockpit. The use of a gunner broke away from the single-seat fighters then in service, returning to the early days of air combat in the First World War with types such as the F.E.2b, F.E.8 and Vickers Gunbus. The difference was now that the gunner was seated behind the pilot and the Bristol Fighter had much better performance and manoeuvrability. After many modifications to the Bristol F.2 prototypes, the F.2a version started operations with a Rolls-Royce (RR) Falcon I, V-12, water-cooled engine giving 190hp. The initial service record of the F.2a – by now known to its crews as either the 'Brisfit' or the 'Biff' – was not good. But that was more the fault of the tactics dictated by HQs and frozen guns caused by the insistence of the engineers that they be liberally oiled. This practice, which came from Army field operations, did not work when the aircraft flew above the freezing level!

By now Bristol had developed the fighter further, incorporating the much more powerful 275hp RR Falcon III and reshaping the rear fuselage to allow the rear gunner more scope. The modified aircraft became the Bristol F.2b and more than 1,500 would be produced and in service by November 1918. The Brisfit was a favourite with its aircrew and won a deserved reputation as a rugged and effective fighter.

The Shuttleworth Bristol F.2b Fighter was built in 1918 and missed any action during the First World War. However, it did serve with No. 208 Squadron in Turkey during the 1920s; it still carries its original military registration of D8096. In 1936 it was bought as a surplus airframe by Captain C.P.B. Ogilvie with the aim of refurbishing it to flying condition and it was allocated the civil registration G-AEPH. However, nothing further happened until after the Second World War, when the F.2b was acquired by the Bristol Aircraft Company and fully restored. As it did with the Boxkite, it passed D8096 to the Collection, where it has been regularly flown and displayed since 1952. In the early 1980s the aircraft underwent a further refurbishment. The installed 275hp Rolls-Royce Falcon III is possibly the oldest RR engine still operating anywhere in the world.

After flying the S.E.5a, the first impression given by the F.2b is one of lumbering size. Its wingspan is half as much again and its length 25 per cent more than the S.E.5. The wing area of the two-seater is more than a third greater, so that initial impression is valid. Hence the expectation is that flying and displaying the F.2b will perhaps be a bit disappointing. But that may come later; first we have to climb aboard and get that big V-12 engine going. Having walked around to check all the wires and fabric, all that remains is to clamber up the side and get aboard. The first step is a bit of a giant one for a short man! There is a footstep let into the lower left fuselage, much like that on the S.E.5a; however, the Brisfit's signature design feature of the fuselage being set above the lower wing makes it noticeably higher. Once up on the step, the next obstacle is the exhaust pipe, about one-third of the way up to the rim of the large front cockpit. The temptation to step on it en route is great but that should be avoided. So the second step is as big as the first! Once over the top it is relatively easy to swing around. If you find yourself facing the tail you set off with the wrong foot! All is not lost, there's plenty of room to turn round and settle onto the wicker seat mounted on top of a box, which is actually the rear fuel tank. I'm not sure I would have wanted to go into mortal combat sitting on 19 gallons of high octane petrol with no parachute!

After the cosiness of the S.E.5 cockpit, the Bristol's width and depth come as a bit of a surprise, but not altogether a pleasant one. I get a feeling that I won't have the intimate connection with the aeroplane as I do with the S.E.5. A bowed, structural metal strut that lies across the cockpit between me and the instrument panel does nothing to allay this feeling. Then, when I look outside from my seated position, I wonder how those magnificent men managed to fight so successfully – the overall view was obstructed in most directions by the upper wing, multiple struts and the rather high engine cowling of the Falcon. The only clear view I had was dead ahead between the upper wing and the nose; not bad for sighting the Vickers gun. *It might be better in flight*, I thought.

The rather distant instrument panel was well furnished with all the usual instruments, most of them contemporary models; plus similar brass piping as in the S.E.5 for the fuel and air pressure systems. In addition to the throttle, in its conventional position on the left cockpit wall, were two other collocated levers: mixture and advance/retard. The latter was new to me in an aviation context. However, as I had once owned a 1934, 6-litre, Lagonda motor car

I knew what that shiny lever did and how it operated.* Also down on the left was the fuel tank selector lever: the 26-gallon 'front' tank was behind the engine and I was sitting on the 'rear' one. The fuel system was furnished with both a hand-pump and primer pump; a similarity with the S.E.5.

The starting procedures were pretty normal, with the exception that I checked that the advance/retard lever was set aft – fully retarded. Like the S.E.5, the Bristol was equipped with a starter magneto and this time it was my job to wind it. It was usual to have the prop swung, although the Collection's Hucks Starter could be used. (More on that rather Heath Robinson device later.) Because of the size of the engine, two brave chaps were 'volunteered' to swing the prop: one to pull on the prop and the other to pull on him! It was very important to get the co-ordination right – especially in NOT winding the starter magneto until the prop had turned through at least 30 degrees.** However, in my experience the Falcon was a dream to start – it seemed to fire first time every time. Once it was going it was important to set about 800rpm. Below this and grumbling noises would emanate from the backlash in the reduction gearbox – above would run the risk of the engine heating up too quickly and unevenly. Like the S.E.5, the temperature of the Falcon was controlled by the setting of 'Venetian blind' radiator shutters.

Assuming that all was well, the magnetos had been checked and one-third advance timing set, then it was time to move off. The standard procedure for the Bristol Fighter was to use 'wing walkers' to help steer and, if necessary, hold back the aircraft on the way out to the runway. The lack of brakes and the rather unpredictable behaviour of the sprung tailskid, which tended to wobble from side to side, made it much safer to not move about the airfield independently. Actually the ride was quite good, although the long wings and narrow track undercarriage did cause a rather unseemly wallowing gait over rough patches!

At the take-off point, with fully advanced timing and neutral elevator trim set, it is time to swing onto the runway and apply full power. The motor

---

* The timing of the spark generated by the spark plugs is crucial to efficient operation of a reciprocating engine. In the early days that function was not automatic as it is now. Thus pilots and drivers were given the capability to control the timing with a control lever; this allowed the instant of the ignition of the fuel to be made earlier (advanced) or later (retarded).

** The danger being that winding the starter mag too early could cause the prop to move rapidly in the wrong direction, so possibly injuring the prop swinger – never a popular move!

wound up to just over 2,000rpm without any fuss and no sooner had I got the aircraft running straight than it lifted off with virtually no change in attitude, at what felt like a very low airspeed; we just soared effortlessly aloft. Homesick angels came to mind!

Up and away the Brisfit gives the impression of a purposeful fighting machine. Although the ailerons get very heavy above 90mph, the relative precision of control in pitch makes it a pleasure to manoeuvre at speeds less than that. As expected, co-ordinated rudder is essential when rolling and sideslips are easily generated at approach speeds around 70–80mph. The stall is very conventional with a distinctive nose-down pitch break at 45mph; although I did get the impression that the rudder was close to having zero effect. As aerobatics were not allowed I practised some wingovers and steep turns. It was obvious that the impressive turn rate and small turn radius at speeds between 70 and 90mph would be major elements of a display and that these characteristics undoubtedly helped the Bristol Fighter gain its reputation as a formidable combatant. The only drawback was that the view into the turns was poor because of the upper wing,

I had been briefed that landing could be tricky if it was not directly into wind. Those First World War aviators often had circular airfields so that problem was easily avoided. The approach is a bit of a balancing act between keeping the engine temperature up while it is throttled back, and reducing the speed from 65 progressively to 50 just before touchdown. Obviously the radiators can be closed, but a trickle of power is ideal so a steep approach angle should be avoided. Those big square wings still give lots of lift at landing speed, so in calm conditions the big fighter tends to float like a butterfly. But once down it can sting like a bee! With its relatively narrow track undercart, heaviness at the back end and the wobbly tailskid, it is prone to ground-loop. The saving grace is that once it does settle fully onto the grass all that weight and drag makes it stop quickly. Then the wonderful wing walkers will turn up to guide us back to our parking space.

It took me more than one flight to feel at home in the Bristol Fighter. However, it is one aeroplane that grows on you. It is like a big, smooth, friendly dog – a powerful pull, untiring friendliness and durability. While it doesn't possess the sprightliness and terrier-like qualities of the smaller single-seat fighters, I could see why the pilots and gunners of the RFC and RAF liked its trustworthiness and why it served for almost twenty years – much longer than most of its 1917 contemporaries.

Vampire T.11 WZ419. (Peter R. March)

Canberra B(I)8. (Peter R. March)

The Red Devils' Islander taking off from Queen's Parade, Aldershot. (FAST via Phil Catling)

Boeing B-17 *Sally B.* (Peter R. March)

The author flying the DH.51 and Gordon McClymont in DH Gipsy Moth G-ABAG at Old
Warden on 20 May 1995. (Steven Jefferson)

DH.60 Moth G–EBLV. (Steven Jefferson)

DH Tiger Moth. (Steven Jefferson)

S.E.5a F904. (Steven Jefferson)

The author making a waving, low, slow flypast in the Miles Magister at Old Warden on 9 July 1996. (Author's collection)

The DHC Chipmunk flying 'round the bend' at Old Warden. (Steven Jefferson)

BA Swallow. (Steven Jefferson)

Swallow cockpit. (Steven Jefferson)

Granger Archaeopteryx. Note pilot's hand on the throttle outside the cockpit! (Steven Jefferson)

Mignet 'Flying Flea'; pilot in correct headgear! (Steven Jefferson)

Avro Rota. I'm smiling but I can't see a thing ahead! (Steven Jefferson)

Miles Hawk Speed 6. (Steven Jefferson)

DH.88 Comet Racer *Grosvenor House*; note the appalling forward view! (Steven Jefferson)

Hawker Hind. (Steven Jefferson)

Gloster Gladiator flown by George Ellis photographed from the Chipmunk, flown by the author on 6 May 1990. (Author's collection)

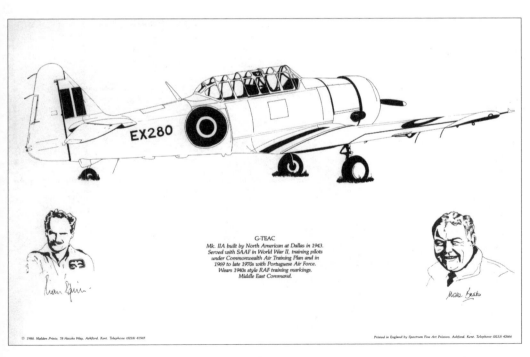

G-TEAC
Mk. IIA built by North American at Dallas in 1943.
Served with SAAF in World War II, training pilots
under Commonwealth Air Training Plan and in
1969 to late 1970s with Portuguese Air Force.
Wears 1940s style RAF training markings.
Middle East Command.

Drawings of the late Euan English, his Harvard (G-TEAC) and the author. (Author's collection)

HFT Harvard during a display. (Steven Jefferson)

The Harvard's broken fuel selector valve and HFT badge. (Author's collection)

Hunter G–BOOM coming in to land. (PRM Aviation Collection)

Mike and Linda Brooke leaving the 1991 DH Moth Rally at Woburn Abbey in Terry Bucket's Moth Minor Coupé G-AFNG. (Author's collection)

11

Trainers

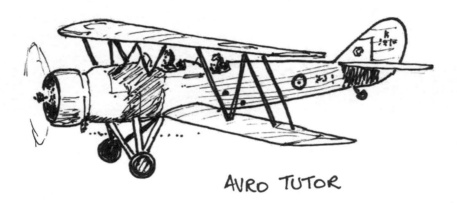

AVRO TUTOR

Apart from the very earliest pioneers and various other beachcombers on the shores of aviation, there has long been a need for aeroplanes to carry more than one person – the pilot – either as a means of teaching other would-be aviators how to do it, or to be able to share the pleasure of flying. The Collection has several aircraft in one or other of these categories, apart from the various DH Moths.

The first British military trainer that was built and used in large numbers was developed from the Avro 504, which first flew in 1913 and soon formed the backbone of RFC and the RAF flying training for the following twenty years. The Collection owns and flies a 504K; in fact, it not only participates in displays but also operates in the training role for the conversion of Collection pilots to the peculiarities of operating rotary engines. When offered the choice of moving onto the rotary-engined part of the Shuttleworth air fleet, or flying the 'heavy metal', with such aircraft as the Hawker Hind, Gloster Gladiator or Supermarine Spitfire on offer, I chose the latter. Thus the oldest, purpose-built military trainer that I flew was the Hawker Tomtit.

Hawker Tomtit G-AFTA (K1786)

In 1927 the Hawker Aircraft Company responded to an Air Ministry requirement for an RAF trainer to replace the latest version of the Avro 504. The Ministry specified that the powerplant should be the radial, five-cylinder, Armstrong Siddeley Mongoose engine, and, in order to expand the national metal-working expertise, the design should 'have regards to the elimination of the woodworking fitter trades'. In other words, the airframe, though not its covering, had to be manufactured using metal. Hence Hawker's Chief Designer, Sydney Camm, designed the Tomtit, a biplane with a frame made of steel and duralumin tubes and fabric covered. Automatic slats of the Handley Page type were fitted to the leading edges of the upper wing, the engine was uncowled and the Tomtit had fixed mainwheels and tailskid. The instructor and trainee sat in open tandem cockpits. The rear cockpit was provided with the then new blind flying instrument panel and a retractable cockpit hood so that blind flying instruction was possible. The RAF Tomtits were fitted with 150hp Mongoose IIIC motors. The prototype was first flown by Hawker chief test pilot George Bulman in November 1928. Twenty-four Tomtits were delivered to the RAF for evaluation. In the event, Avro won the contract with its Tutor. However, the Tomtit marked the start of Hawker's entry into the metal, fabric-covered military aeroplane genre, with the Hart, Hind and Hurricane being some of the many models produced over the following ten or more years. Hawker also produced five civil-registered Tomtits.

The Collection's Tomtit was the last off the production line and is the only known survivor. It has an interesting history, as it was used by test pilot and pre-war air racer Alex Henshaw as a 'hack' to fly between aircraft production locations. One day at Old Warden I had the great honour to be introduced and chat with him for a while.* I was astonished how young and alive he

---

* Alex Henshaw, MBE (7 November 1912–24 February 2007) was a British air racer in the 1930s and a test pilot for Vickers Armstrong during the Second World War. In my opinion his books *Sigh for a Merlin* (1979) and *The Flight of the Mew Gull* (1980) are 'must-reads' for all aviation enthusiasts.

looked for an octogenarian; I am to this day equally astonished that all he received for his unstinting and rigorous work as a test pilot throughout the Second World War was an MBE.

After moving through another pair of hands, G-AFTA ended up being owned by another renowned test pilot, Neville Duke, who flew it in air displays and races. In 1950 it was acquired by Hawker Aircraft and, in 1956, handed over to the Shuttleworth Collection for preservation in flying condition. At that time the Tomtit was finished in an attractive dark blue and gold, which were, incidentally, the racing colours of HRH Princess Margaret. In 1967 the aircraft was repainted in the original RAF silver livery and markings.

The Tomtit is an attractive-looking aircraft and sits on the ground with a forward-leaning attitude, as if it is eager to go flying. This impression comes from the rather large forward displacement, or stagger, of the upper wing and the wheels sitting under the leading edge of the lower wing. The wing stagger is there to allow the front seat occupant, should it be necessary, to make a clean and easy parachute exit. Like the vast majority of two-seat biplanes, the Tomtit is flown solo from the rear seat. Unsurprisingly, one of the cautionary words I received before my first flight was that the Tomtit is very light on its wheels and care must be taken not to allow the tail to come up prematurely.

Having admired its looks and checked all around, it is time to climb aboard; this is very easy (for a change) as footsteps are provided and the rim of the cockpit is barely 4ft from the ground. The cockpit is roomy and neatly laid out. There is one additional and useful feature that was quite a novelty for its time – the seat is adjustable for height; something this pilot very much appreciated! Nevertheless, the view ahead on the ground is, as expected, not good. I am instantly impressed with the instrument panel and the way that all the controls, switches and levers are where I expect to find them. I feel already that this flight is going to be a real pleasure.

Having checked all the bits that need checking, it is time to get the Mongoose turning. The usual back and forth calls are made to ensure that everything is safe for the motor to be primed. Having been reminded by my friendly groundcrew as to how many strokes on the Kigass primer pump are likely to work today, I first ensure that the pump itself is full of fuel and then count off the strokes. Meanwhile, outside the prop is being pulled over. Now all is ready and the two chaps out front link hands to swing the prop together. In the Tomtit this is done with the main magnetos off and the starter magneto switched on. In order to avoid a premature detonation, and possible dangerous backswing of the prop, the Mongoose is started after a '3-2-1-Now!' countdown from the cockpit. At the 'Now' the men pull as hard as they can and step well back; I wait a couple of seconds and then wind the starter magneto handle madly. With any amount of luck the engine will fire and slowly pick up. Then the main mags are switched on and the starter mag is switched off.

If the engine pick-up is uneven and the prop hesitates, or even momentarily kicks back, it is best to keep turning the handle until correct ignition happens. I had been told that on rare occasions the Mongoose had kept running in reverse and that the only clue was that there was no slipstream over the cockpit. If that was missed then when the chocks were pulled away and the power increased, the little trainer would set off backwards! Although I suspect that was an apocryphal story!

However, today the little round motor is running correctly and I've checked that the all-important oil pressure has risen and set 1,000rpm. But there is nothing smooth about this motor; it is a radial and its single, big-end bearing with its rotating mass give the same feeling as one gets sitting on a large-capacity singe-cylinder motorcycle. It recalls my experience with a single-cylinder 500cc BSA Gold Star in my youth! As I wait for the oil temperature to reach 15°C, I become aware of some soreness on my right hand. The culprit is the starter magneto handle, which is very close to the right cockpit wall and, without gloves, I would probably have skinned my knuckles. I also notice that as I inadvertently move the stick forward while checking other things the tail tries to rise. So when it is time to increase rpm to 1,500 for a check of the magnetos the two erstwhile propeller pullers go aft and lay across the rear fuselage.

After all is checked I wave the chocks away and, thankfully, we move off forwards. With its steerable tailskid and ready response from the engine, the Tomtit proves to be easy to taxi; but I must remember to hold the stick hard back and that there are no brakes.

Having lined up on the runway, I progressively increase power, keeping straight with rudder, and, being quite a lightweight, the aeroplane accelerates nicely. Just relaxing the back pressure on the stick makes the tail come up and the whole aircraft soon follows its example. Once airborne we accelerate readily to 65mph and I adjust the attitude to hold that speed for the climb.

After less than five minutes we are cruising at 3,000ft and 85mph with the engine running smoothly at 1,650rpm; this will give a very economic fuel consumption of 7 gallons per hour. The control in pitch is crisp, precise and light and I predict that the landing should be a relatively unruffled affair. I try rolling into a turn and find only a modest rate of roll, although the forces are not high, as on some other biplanes. However, as soon as aileron was applied very noticeable sideslip followed. Further tests on the directional stability show it to be very weak; the Tomtit needs a bigger tail! Forewarned is forearmed, so I use rudder liberally to minimise slip during various rolling manoeuvres. Before trying out some aerobatics, I set up for a straight stall. I use the controls to keep a slow, sideslip-free, steady deceleration; there are no worrying control issues and the gentle stall occurs at a speed below the minimum shown on the ASI – about 45mph. The minimum speed for landing will be 55.

The maximum speed allowed is 130mph, so I set full throttle and accelerate in level flight to see what she'll do. We reach 100mph quite quickly and then I lower the nose to accelerate further, throttling back a little to hold the rpm below its maximum allowed value of 2,035rpm. At 130mph there is no excessive vibration or other worrying symptoms, although the gale around my head is getting quite unpleasant. I raise the nose smoothly and fly into a loop. It goes round well but I have to use the rudder to keep the loop vertical. I then fly a few wingovers and steep turns as practice for displays and finally try a barrel roll. The latter goes better than I expected by dint of achieving a high nose attitude and using full aileron and lots of balancing rudder over the top. Any other rolls with negative G are off-limits so I decide that it's now time to go home.*

As I descend I become aware that the natural turbulence on this fine summer's day is showing up the Tomtit's only deficiency. The little aeroplane snakes about, wagging its tail in response to the bumps. There is not much roll response so any corrections are made with the rudder. I make a note that displays on bumpy days might be a bit more restrained.

Back at Old Warden, turning onto the final approach at 65mph the Tomtit feels good. I am now fully aware of the need to keep active on the rudder and that the ailerons are not powerful, but that is all compensated by the precise handling in pitch and responsive engine. All of which adds up to a very pleasant experience – so different from the trepidation more often felt in this phase of flight in some other aircraft; especially when being watched by several thousand members of the public and flying the world's only example!

---

* At the time the Tomtit was not banned from basic aerobatic manoeuvres. The CAA undertook a review in about 1996 and withdrew the permission for aerobatics from many of the Collection's aerobatic-capable aircraft.

Once over the end of the runway at 55mph the aeroplane can be brought to the ground with precision and little effort. The only thing to remember is that the directional control is now down to the tailskid. But the low touch-down speed and grass surface mean that we are at walking speed in quite a short distance and the aircraft is easy to control for clearing the runway and taxying back.

The Tomtit is a good one. Apart from not having quite enough tail surface, Sydney Camm did a great and pioneering job. I flew several displays in the Tomtit and I much preferred it to the Tiger Moth. The Tomtit is more purposeful, better equipped and, to my mind, would have been a much better trainer for its generation of radial-engined biplanes, such as the Bristol Bulldog and the Gloster Gamecock. More importantly, on a personal note, it was a privilege to fly such a delightful inter-war flying machine; especially as it is the only one left.

Avro Tutor – G-AHSA (K3215)

At around the same time that Hawker's Tomtit was being considered for RAF service, Avro designed a replacement for its very successful 504 series of trainers. It was known as the Model 621 and was a private venture conceived as an initial pilot trainer. The biplane featured staggered, equal-span, single-bay wings and a rather long, well-sprung undercarriage with tailskid; later models had a tailwheel. The construction was based on a frame of steel tubing (with some wooden components in the wing ribs) and a doped linen covering. This aircraft was initially named the Avro Trainer, so giving everyone a clear indication of its proposed role! The first flight of the prototype, G-AAKT, took place in September 1929, piloted by Avro chief test pilot Captain 'Sam' Brown. Like the Tomtit, the Avro 621 was powered by an Armstrong Siddeley Mongoose and sported the long, high aspect ratio wings that marked its Avro pedigree. Further development of the Trainer followed, mainly through the replacement of the Mongoose with the Armstrong Siddeley Lynx; a seven-cylinder, radial engine giving 240hp. This model was named the Tutor and became the standard production variant. More than 600 Tutors were built, many of them for overseas air forces.

The Tutor marked a step improvement in the equipment of military trainers. It had a tailwheel and mainwheel brakes. The cockpits were spacious and the seats and the rudder pedals could be adjusted for height and reach. The Tutor was also equipped with ailerons on both upper and lower wings, which gave it much better roll performance than any of its predecessors, and it had a variable incidence tailplane for longitudinal trimming. The relatively large and more powerful engine offered more relevant handling for preparation to fly the operational aircraft of the day.

As with the Tomtit, the Shuttleworth Collection Avro Tutor is the sole surviving example of the type still flying. It is known that K3215 served at the RAF College at Cranwell from 1933 to 1936, when it was transferred to the Central Flying School. It is also believed to be the final Tutor to be retired from the RAF in 1946. After being privately owned for about ten years it was bought by the Collection after it suffered an engine failure while being ground-run for the 1956 film *Reach for the Sky*. It took no fewer than three non-working engines to provide the components for a replacement unit. This work was undertaken by the original manufacturer, Armstrong Siddeley, at its Coventry base. Sadly, further engine problems occurred in 1979 and a worldwide search failed to discover another Lynx. The aircraft is flying today due to a painstaking rebuild in the early 1980s by a member of the Old Warden engineering team.

I first flew the Avro Tutor on Saturday, 16 May 1992; it was my 100th aircraft type. When I parked, I found that my lovely lady Linda had let the cat out of the bag and Peter Symes, the general manager, was there with glasses of bubbly! At the time the Tutor was finished in an overall yellow paint scheme carrying the crane (bird) logo of the RAF College Cranwell. Although possessed of a blunt-nosed bulk, the Tutor gave off an air of purposeful, handsome ruggedness.

Getting aboard was easier than many of its contemporaries, especially to the usual rear cockpit. Two inset steps were provided so that, as long as one set off with the correct foot, swinging into the roomy cockpit posed no difficulty. Both cockpits were well furnished and more or less identical. The only slight problem with flying solo was that the magneto switches in the front cockpit worked in series, so they had to be switched on by the groundcrew after engine priming had been completed. One new control lever was present that I had not come across before. That was the locking lever for the automatic slats on the outer parts of the upper wing. This was used to lock the slats in when on the ground, presumably to reduce wear and tear as they would otherwise bob in and out as one taxied. Starting, using a starter mag operated from the rear cockpit, was identical to the Tomtit.

Two burly chaps on the prop – '3-2-1-Now!' etc. Moreover, the Lynx was as prone to backfiring and running in reverse as the Mongoose! After starting it was very important to make sure that the oil pressure came up promptly. As the engine was also the only one of its type left, we took extremely good care of it.

The use of the brakes and castoring tailwheel made directional control on the ground a doddle, even in a good breeze. On take-off the Tutor was not unlike the Bristol Fighter in that it tended to levitate airborne at a speed slightly below that expected. Once free of the drag of *terra firma* the big bird accelerated well and I could throttle back from around 1,800 to 1,700rpm for the climb at 70mph; I reckoned the climb rate to be about 800ft per minute. Although at this speed the responses in pitch and roll were not crisp, the Tutor demonstrated moderate stability. However, like many aircraft of the day, if the rudder pedals were released then the rudder bar took itself off to hide in a corner – the Tutor was directionally statically unstable with power on.

At my chosen height of 4,000ft I levelled off; with 1,600rpm on the motor the aircraft accelerated to and settled at 90mph. The first thing that I noticed was how windy it was in the cockpit – much more so than the other similar types that I'd flown. At this speed the response in roll was much better and the control of attitude with the elevator equally good. However, the longitudinal static stability was quite strong, so much use had to be made of the large elevator trimwheel, which fell readily to hand: my left hand. Holding straight and level flight and throttling back resulted in a fairly rapid deceleration, so I lowered the nose a little to see what would happen as we approached the stall. At 55mph the controls started to feel woolly and at about 45mph the nose dropped, despite my efforts to hold it up. There seemed to be no tendency for a wing to drop and the whole event presented no undue problems. The recovery on applying full throttle and forward stick was immediate and the loss of height minimal. Perhaps the Tutor was a bit too docile in this respect for a trainer? Of course, in the cause of preservation, we didn't spin it, but I imagined that the Tutor would behave immaculately in both entry and recovery from such an event.

The Tutor was another of the Collection's aircraft that, at the time, we were allowed to aerobat, so that was next before I flew back to Old Warden. The maximum permitted speed was 140mph, so I thought that 120 would be a good start speed for a loop. I picked a safe area to fly into and checked that the sky around me appeared otherwise unoccupied, adopted a shallow dive and applied full throttle. The speed rose to 120mph and I pulled up. The speed then fell rapidly so I pulled back as far as I dare and toppled over the top in a most unsatisfactory manner. I repositioned for another try but added 10mph. From 130mph, using the minimum amount of G that I could, the Tutor surprised me by flying round a nice vertical and fairly round loop – what a difference 10mph made! I followed that with a wingover in each direction from 110mph and a barrel roll from 120. All seemed satisfactory so, having inflicted sufficient exercise on this rare airframe and engine, I closed the throttle and adopted a descending attitude to achieve the recommended gliding speed of 70mph. I held this for about 1,000ft, which took just less than a minute, and then gently opened the throttle to warm the engine, before resuming the descent to 1,000ft above the airfield. It was my invariable habit to spend at least a couple of minutes gliding so that should the engine ever fail I would know what it looked like and how far I could go before circling to land, hopefully in a suitable field. One of the lessons in the Tutor was dealing with the large trim change from higher speeds to lower.

Back in the circuit this lesson would be applied in that lots of nose-up trim would be required before landing. Having flown downwind at 80mph to just past abeam the end of the runway, I set a trickle of power and turned toward a short final approach, allowing the speed to come back to 70mph in the turn and then, at about 300ft, reducing towards 55 'over the hedge'. Despite the large, round nose the view ahead, until the very last stages, was quite adequate. The actual landing was not taxing and the large, soft under-carriage complemented even the roughest of touch-downs. The lack of drag from the tailwheel, unlike that from a skid, meant that it may be necessary to use the brakes, but on most occasions the weight and natural drag of the whole aeroplane brought it to walking pace fairly quickly.

I flew several displays in the Tutor at Old Warden; however, one day I received a phone call from Chris Morris, the chief engineer. He asked whether I might be free on the weekend of 23 and 24 June 1995 to take the Tutor away for a display at the original Avro airfield near Woodford in Cheshire. I said that I would, so I drew some lines on a map and calculated the time and fuel usage; the normal consumption at 90mph was 11 gallons per hour. The Tutor's 30-gallon tank should therefore allow a safe two and a half hours transit; this trip should take less than two hours. I also got hold of the approach plates for Woodford aerodrome, as I knew that it was inside the Manchester Control Zone (CTZ). On Saturday, 23 June I arrived at Old Warden pretty well prepared and received a briefing and authorisation from the chief pilot. One thing that bothered me was that a radio could not be fitted. However, I need not have worried. An arrangement had been made for a radio-equipped light aircraft from Woodford to meet me just north-east of Crewe at 3 p.m.; it would escort me to Woodford.

I calculated that I needed to depart at 1.30 p.m., before the start of the afternoon's display. After a light lunch I climbed aboard the big, yellow bird, well wrapped up for almost two hours in an open cockpit at 3,000ft, where despite it being June the temperature was forecast to be no more than 10°C. Once airborne I followed the line on my map, heading north-west passing outside the Birmingham CTZ, over Cannock Chase, and picking up the M6 motorway leading towards Crewe. All went well, the winds were not too strong and I was able to map-read my way along the track, seeing some very interesting bits of the UK with which I was not that familiar. I arrived at Crewe, which I had easily identified by the multiple railway tracks converging from all directions to the centre of this 'Railway Town'. Having descended to the pre-arranged height of 2,000ft and held over the north-eastern suburbs, I looked around and spotted a high-winged Cessna aircraft not far away, so pointed the Tutor towards it. As I closed in I saw the Cessna's wings waggle, so I waggled back and joined up on his right. Then I just followed him until we were overhead a large airfield at 1,000ft, whereupon he turned rapidly left and left me to make my own arrangements. From the windsock below me I could see that the wind was favouring runway 25 so set myself up to land. I hadn't landed the Tutor on a hard surface before. Knowing that, despite the display being on the following day, there were already lots of folk down there, I concentrated on making a decent fist of the arrival. In the event I didn't bounce too high and followed the waved instructions for parking.

Once I had shut down, remembering to turn off the additional magneto switches in the front cockpit, I asked about overnight parking and refuelling. All was in hand and by the time I had tied the stick in position with the seat straps and put the cover, which had been stowed aboard, over the cockpits, a fuel truck had arrived and we topped off the tank. The forecast for the overnight period was for less than 10kt winds, so there was no need to tie the aircraft down; just put the brakes on and chocks in.

The following day two Shuttleworth 'volunteers' had arrived, complete with oil and a few tools; this was good as I didn't have to brief anyone else for the pre-start and prop swinging duties. My display was due to be early enough to allow me to fly the ten-minute slot, land to collect my bag and maps and depart towards the end of the afternoon. The display went well enough, with a couple of aerobatics, wingovers, steep turns and low flypasts for the photographers.

The return journey was memorable for two things. About halfway back, north-east of Birmingham, I needed to refold my map and while doing so the constant strong and buffeting airflow in the cockpit snatched it from my hands and it disappeared over the side! The other equally dire memory I have of that trip was the cold. The temperature at 3,000ft during the early evening had probably dropped to near freezing and after over an hour I was getting very cold. And I still had about forty-five minutes more to go. I tried lowering the seat and leaning forward, which took me out of the worst of the gale, but I needed to look over the side to see where I was going, so it was a bit counter-productive! Eventually I found my way back in the gathering gloom of a cloudy evening and was very thankful to land safely, in good order, shut down and get the aeroplane put to bed. Now it was my turn to drive home, with the heater on, and do likewise!

Miles Magister M.14A – G-AJRS (P6382)

In 1936 the Air Ministry issued a requirement for a monoplane trainer to prepare pilots for the new fighters about to enter RAF service, such as the Hawker Hurricane, Supermarine Spitfire and Fairey Battle. The Miles Aircraft Company responded with a development of its very successful line of monoplane racers – a model it called the Trainer; as in Avro's predecessor to the Tutor, a rather prosaic name! Over time the Trainer was developed into a more rugged version for military use and called the Magister. In keeping with Miles' practice, it was an all-wooden, low-wing monoplane with tandem open cockpits, and it made its first flight on 20 March 1937 with no less a personage than the firm's founder, Mr F.G. Miles, at the controls. The 'Maggie', as it quickly became known, was powered by the ubiquitous DH Gipsy Major engine giving 130hp to a fixed-pitch, two-bladed propeller. The first deliveries to the RAF started in September of 1937. The Maggie was equipped with a tailwheel, brakes to the mainwheels and vacuum-operated flaps. By the end of its production run no fewer than 1,303 Magisters had been built. After the war 148 Maggies were released from military service and were civil-registered as Miles Trainer IIIs. In the mid-1950s the Air Registration Board (the CAA's predecessor), being mistrustful of old wooden aeroplanes, withdrew their blessing and many were scrapped. Today there are three airworthy Magisters in the world. The Shuttleworth Magister was rebuilt using components from two other airframes.

After flying lots of biplanes, progression to the Magister brings an odd sensation of modernity, despite its late 1930s vintage. As I walk up to it, soft helmet and goggles swinging from my right hand, the yellow and camouflage wood panelling gives it a smooth and solid look. No more hints of the internal structure-supporting fabric. The Maggie is quite good looking, although the rather spindly, bare undercarriage legs are not so pretty. The original models had large, streamlined spats, but these were removed after repeated problems of divots of grass and mud getting in and inadvertently braking the wheels; hardly desirable on take-off!

Climbing aboard is very easy using the walkway on the starboard wing root and entering the well laid out cockpit through a drop-down door panel. One of the nice things about the Maggie is that its centre of gravity range is such that, unlike its predecessors, one can fly it solo from the front seat. The first and rather odd thing that I remember noticing was how thick the control column felt; I have fairly small hands so the effect was probably a bit exaggerated. The instrument panel was laid out sensibly and furnished with mostly contemporary dials and indicators. The mouthpiece for the Gosport Tube, used in pre-radio days for communication between the cockpits, was still there.*

The Magister carries 21 gallons of fuel in two tanks, one in each wing root, and the desired tank is selected with a lever in the cockpit. There are fuel gauges in the top of each tank but they are virtually unreadable from the cockpit! For our flying at the Collection it was sufficient to ensure that each tank was full, using the built-in dipsticks, and then fly our short display sorties on one tank. The fuel is drawn from the tanks by two engine-driven pumps and one of them can be operated manually for priming the engine before start-up.

The prop is hand swung and in addition to the usual checks, the flaps are operated. The flap lever has three positions: 'up', 'down' and 'neutral'. The flaps move at a rapid rate and it is very difficult to stop them at any intermediate position. I soon decided to treat the Maggie like my old Canberra and just use the two extremes. Once the differential brakes are set, taxying

---

* A Gosport Tube was a voice pipe used by instructors in the early days of military aviation to give instructions and directions to their students. It was invented at the School of Special Flying at Gosport, Hampshire in 1917.

out to the runway is easy, even in winds of up to 15kt. Although sitting on a tailwheel, the view ahead is much better than, say, the Tiger Moth, but it is still advisable to keep weaving the nose to clear the area directly ahead.

The take-off, made with the flaps up, is straightforward, although perhaps a little more prolonged an affair than I had expected. However, once up and away, climbing at 70mph with 2,100rpm on the Gipsy Major, the Magister climbs at about 700ft per minute. A fair amount of rudder is needed to keep straight. After levelling off and setting the maximum continuous rpm of 2,050, we get a speed of 120mph, which isn't bad for an aeroplane of its design and age. Although the front cockpit is open, the windscreen gives much better protection than many others of the vintage; although I was told that the rear cockpit is much draughtier!

The Maggie flies a bit like a coupé Chipmunk. With 1,900rpm it will cruise happily at 110mph, as opposed to the Chipmunk's 90kt (104mph), giving a fuel consumption of a mere 6½ gallons per hour. That means a safe endurance of around three hours and a range of about 330 statute miles. Like most trainers, the Magister exhibits good longitudinal stability, which helps in teaching students the importance of trimming, but not too much to inhibit manoeuvring. The roll rate is not sparkling, but is much better than the Tiger Moth, and the control forces acceptable, but increasing with speed. The maximum speed of 160mph (limited by the top reading on the airspeed indicator and the desire to preserve the aeroplane) can be reached only in a dive, during which an eye has to be kept on the rpm so that it is not allowed to exceed the maximum permitted value of 2,350. We did not aerobat or spin the Maggie (preservation again) but steep turns and wingovers were permitted during displays. There were no control or stability problems and the usual amounts of rudder with roll were necessary to stay in balance. However, using rudder to sideslip the aircraft reveals a not so desirable characteristic of the Magister.

Starting a sideslip to lose excess height, by applying rudder while holding the wings level, brings about a very strong nose-down trim change. More rudder begets more nose-down force, which must be resisted with back stick. Eventually, and especially with the flaps down, the nose-down moment cannot be stopped. If the rudder is released at this point there is a rapid nose-up movement. Hence, for flight safety reasons, sideslipping on the approach with the flaps down is strictly *verboten*!

The stall with the flaps up occurred at just over 50mph; at around 55mph there was a bit of pre-stall buffet over the tail, felt through the stick and airframe. It seemed difficult to avoid one of the wings (usually the right) dropping rapidly as the nose dropped. Whether this was a vagary of P6382 or Maggies in general I don't know. Oddly with the flaps down, when the stall speed was about 45mph, the wing drop was less likely to happen. When operating the flaps, which were very fast acting, one had to remember the low limiting speed of 75mph. Displays in the Maggie were always delightful as it slipped readily through the air and low passes at 130mph with a steep turn 'around the bend' seemed to be much appreciated. I also used to throw in a slow (70mph), flaps down flypast while waving to the crowd. On 7 July 1996, I flew a formation display alongside one of the other surviving Maggies. It was quite a sight to see two of these now rare birds in the air together.

Landing the Maggie is easier than the old, flapless biplanes and is more in line with modern techniques. The view is excellent and once the flaps are down, the elevator trim set and the 70mph final turn complete, it is easy to use a bit of power to control the flight path angle and the stick to bring the speed back towards 65, falling to 60 'over the hedge'. The round out to the three-point attitude feels less than the biplanes. There is a slight tendency for the aircraft to float if the speed is a few mph too high, the flaps enhancing the ground effect; this could be a problem in a crosswind. I only tried a flapless landing once, practising for a vacuum pump failure, and with a touchdown speed about 10kt higher we did use a lot more of the grass runway, but still stopped with room to spare.

Overall the Magister was the right aircraft for its role and time. The fact that more than 1,300 were built and used to train countless future fighter and bomber pilots for the RAF, the RN and Commonwealth air forces proves its worth. It's such a shame that more of them haven't survived to fly today.

De Havilland Canada DHC-1 Chipmunk
G-AOTD (WB588)

Immediately following the conclusion of the Second World War, there was a desire in Canadian aviation circles to take advantage of the recently expanded aircraft manufacturing industry. Hence it was decided to embark on developing aircraft to replace designs that were now obsolete. De Havilland

Aircraft of Canada Ltd (DHC) was interested in developing indigenous aircraft designs and chose to focus on producing a new pilot training aircraft, specifically as a successor to the DH Tiger Moth.

Wsiewołod Jakimiuk, a naturalised Polish engineer, was the principal designer and led the development of the new aircraft, which became known as the Chipmunk. He designed a cantilevered monoplane that incorporated numerous advances over typical trainer aircraft then in service. These included an enclosed cockpit, brakes and flaps. The Chipmunk prototype, CF-DIO-X, first flew on 22 May 1946 at Downsview, Toronto, piloted by Pat Fillingham, a DH test pilot who had been seconded from the parent company at Hatfield. The prototype was powered by a 145hp DH Gipsy Major 1C air-cooled, piston engine. This was replaced in the production version of the Chipmunk by a 145hp in-line DH Gipsy Major 8 engine.

The Shuttleworth Collection's Chipmunk was ex-RAF WB588 acquired in 1981 after being donated by the RAE. It was restored to flying condition over ten years by a volunteer group from BAe Kingston, and was finished in the colours of Oxford University Air Squadron; the alma mater of the chief pilot of the time. The Chipmunk was sold on in October 1994, when the Shuttleworth air fleet was being rationalised. As those who have read my book *Follow Me Through* may recall, I spent five years as an RAF flying instructor flying the Chipmunk and amassed about 1,200 hours in the little trainer. Hence, at Shuttleworth it was one of the first aircraft that I displayed.

The Chipmunk is a delightful light aircraft to fly and its handling finally corrects those failings that were evident in its predecessors. I was allowed to do aerobatic displays and I used to start at 1,000ft with a loop and then follow that with a series of stall turns, wingovers, and, on a good day, a slow roll. Because it is almost impossible to hold height in the Chipmunk during aerobatics, I would finish with a barrel roll, which I flew down to 200ft or so to start a series of low flypasts for the photographers. One of the things I enjoyed about flying the 'Chippie' at Old Warden was that I didn't need to fly wearing a helmet and goggles; it wasn't often that one could fly bareheaded at Shuttleworth!

12

Tourers

PARNALL ELF

In Britain, the inter-war years of the 1920s and '30s saw unprecedented changes to the social order and the technology of travel. These two decades started with euphoric relief at the end of the First World War; the conflict that, at least initially, was dubbed the 'war to end all wars'. The two decades ended with the darkening horizon of the approach and arrival of another war.

During the first of those terrible conflicts, the development of flying machines accelerated so much that by the Armistice of 1918, aircraft could fly further, faster, higher and carry more than ever before. There were only ten and a half years between the first British heavier-than-air flight that covered a distance of 1,390ft (420m)* and the first Transatlantic crossing covering 1,890 miles (3,040km) in fifteen hours fifty-seven minutes at an

---

* By Samuel F. Cody in his British Army Aeroplane No. 1 at Farnborough on 16 October 1908.

average speed of 115mph.* Speeds approaching 200mph were achievable by many fighters and on 14 June 1919 Jean Casale reached an altitude of 31,230ft in a French Nieuport NiD 29 single-engine fighter.

The end of hostilities had led to a sudden downturn in aircraft production and the laying-off of tens of thousands of skilled workers. Initially the majority of continuing aviation activity revolved around the conversion and modification of surplus military types. However, the expertise that had grown rapidly during the war years was dispersed across the nation. In an atmosphere of social and financial instability, aircraft manufacturers realigned their design and production to civil aircraft for a variety of uses. One of these specialisations was in the production of touring aircraft, designed for the *nouveau riche* to indulge their new-found freedom of the skies. The first British manufacturer to move into volume production was de Havilland with their many Moths. However, alongside them a plethora of individuals exercised their draughtsmanship and started to design and manufacture aircraft for the private market that were primarily aimed at the 'aerial tourist'.

De Havilland DH.51 G-EBIR – 1924

If one looks at Geoffrey de Havilland's military designs for the Royal Flying Corps, the two-seat DH.4 and DH.9, developed as aerial reconnaissance and bomber aircraft, one can spot the fundamental design similarities to the DH.51. Each is a two-bay biplane with a fixed, two-wheel, sprung undercarriage and tailskid and the majority of the structure is wood covered with doped fabric. The DH.51 was scaled down on those models by about 10 per cent in most respects and was modified to allow two passengers to sit in a cockpit ahead of the pilot, who occupied a separate cockpit behind them. The DH.51 was designed as an economical touring machine for the private owner. Initially the prototype G-EBIM, which first flew in July 1924, was fitted with a 90hp war surplus RAF 1a engine, but for various reasons this proved inadequate and difficult to certify. However, three months later G-EBIM flew with a 120hp Airdisco V-8 engine and received civil certification. Although docile enough for the private owner, not many orders were

---

* By John Alcock and John W. Brown in a Vickers Vimy bomber on 14–15 June 1919.

forthcoming and production ceased after just three DH.51s had been built. It seems likely that the costs of owning this rather large private aircraft outweighed the perceived benefits.

G-EBIM went to Australia in April 1927, where it was fitted with floats and operated around Sydney until 1931, when it was destroyed in a landing accident. The second DH.51, G-EBIQ, remained in the UK and was operated by an air taxi company until it was scrapped in 1933. The third and final DH.51, G-EBIR, was shipped to Kenya in September 1925 and registered as VP-KAA. It remained in active service there for almost forty years; the aircraft still bears the name *Miss Kenya* in remembrance of this African heritage. In 1965 it was air freighted to the UK and restored by Hawker Siddeley Aviation at Hawarden in Cheshire. In 1972 *Miss Kenya* was flown to Old Warden and placed in the permanent care of the Collection. It is still flying today, more than ninety years since it was built.

There are a couple of oddities in the cockpit, the first being that the stick is furnished with a fighter-like spade-grip handle; the second is that there are no instruments on the panel immediately in front of the pilot. Instead there is a hinged flap, over a circular aperture through which the pilot can communicate with and check on the well-being of the passengers! There is a third item that bears mention: the ignition switches are outside the cockpit on the right. The first time that I flew the DH.51, I discovered that once I had strapped in I could not reach them and had to undo my harness to switch them on before the prop was swung. Next time I strapped in while the engine was warming up!

Starting the relatively beefy engine, with its large, four-bladed propeller, requires the use of two strong men to swing it, along with the procedures allied to using a starter magneto that I've already described. The post-start checks of magnetos and oil pressure are normal for an air-cooled engine; the only thing to bear in mind is that the motor is prone to overheating on the ground, so we will not hang about. However, steering the DH.51, which has no brakes and a rather recalcitrant sprung but unsteerable tailskid, is not easy. It often requires wing-walkers to help with getting round corners or helping to hold the big, eager machine back on a slope.

Take-off, once the tailskid is lined up with the rest of the machine, is very straightforward (literally!) and, in a manner reminiscent of the Bristol Fighter, *Miss Kenya* lifts off in a very ladylike manner. However, with the engine, which is relatively low revving, set at 1,800rpm and 65–70mph the aircraft climbs well, at around 900ft per minute. Up and away the DH.51

not only looks like a big Moth – it flies like one. The stall is benign and the stalling speed is given as 43mph, but that is below the minimum reading on the ASI.

Except in turbulent conditions, the DH.51 is docile and using the normal aileron and rudder technique it can be flown in a display with a modicum of spirit. We often flew the 51 in formations with other DH products and then the difference in size between it and its little brothers and sisters was easy to see. The DH.51 pilot was invariably asked to lead the formations so that the more agile Moths could keep station.

Landing the DH.51 is, as one might expect, like landing a Moth. She sits down well on three points, but is less forgiving if one lands prematurely. The big wing is still producing lift and she will soar aloft and settle back slowly. Crosswinds are to be avoided because that all-moving skid allows the aircraft to easily weathercock into wind. The DH.51 is yet another of the Collections 'only one of its type in the world', so landing safely is always a relief; especially in public! It is, as ever, a privilege to have flown a unique machine; one that, although not a success in its own right, led to the development of the most successful series of British light aircraft – that multitude of Moths.

Parnall Elf G-AAIN – 1929

One of the lesser aircraft design and manufacturing companies that evolved during the First World War was George Parnall & Co. This Bristol-based, wood-working business was primarily a shop-fitting firm, which moved into military aviation construction in 1916. However, Parnall had designed aircraft as early as 1910, although without much success. During the First World War, the skilled staff was moved to sites around Bristol and Gloucestershire, producing aeroplanes to the firm's own designs and, under contract, those of other companies. But in 1920, all Parnall's aircraft-related activity moved to the former RFC airfield at Yate, north-east of Bristol. There Harold Bolas, an aircraft designer who had worked for the British Admiralty's Air Department, joined Parnall and over the next nine years he and his boss, Harris Booth, designed many biplanes, mostly for RAF and RN use. Apart from the Panther, which went into mass production with the Bristol Aircraft Company, not many of the various models were produced in large numbers.*

The Elf was Bolas' final design before he left Parnall to move to the USA. Many of its features follow on from previous designs. In particular the unique 'Warren girder' layout of the vee-shaped wing struts, which removed the need for wire bracing. The fuselage was plywood covered and the wings and control surfaces finished in the usual doped fabric. Like many light aircraft of the time, for storage and towing, the wings were designed to fold back and lock alongside the fuselage. The Elf was fitted with a 105hp Hermes engine and had an unusual fuel system that pumped the fuel from the 18-gallon main tank in the fuselage up into a 3-gallon emergency and feeder tank in the wing centre section. The other unusual feature (and unique in my experience) was the fitment of two elevator trimmers; a wheel and a lever. The latter adjusts the strength of the spring bias and the wheel gives finer control. Another oddity is the terminology connected to these items in that the fully aft (nose-up) position is marked 'stall'!

Three Elfs were made and flown; G-AAIN first flew in 1932 and was bought by Lord Apsley. The other two were destroyed in flying accidents in the mid-1930s. G-AAIN was stored throughout the Second World War and bought by the Collection in non-flying condition in July 1951. After a period on loan to a museum, it was restored to flying condition at Old Warden and made its first public appearance in August 1980. The Shuttleworth Elf is finished in a very attractive dark green and cream colour scheme, with a shiny metal propeller spinner and solid-centred wheels. It gives the appearance of a sleek and sturdy flying machine.

Access to the rear cockpit is not that easy as no footsteps are provided, so it's a bit of a stretch. The front cockpit is fitted with a removable cover, à la DH.51. Once aboard, the cockpit has the usual look and layout for the period. The primary item is to remember to select the main tank on the ground and in flight, and only use the feeder (emergency) tank for take-off and landing. Priming and starting the Hermes is the same as in the Moth and once it is going and we've checked its health we can go aviating. The Elf has a fixed tailskid and taxying is much like a Moth but the weight is 20 per cent higher, so there is more inertia to overcome; it is feasible to move about the airfield without external help in winds up to 10kt.

---

* One hundred and fifty Parnall Panther carrier-borne reconnaissance aircraft were built and delivered to the Royal Navy.

Take-off is a lengthier affair than in a Moth and this sets the scene for the rest of the flight. The Elf does not live up to its sprightly name. The roll rate is disappointing and rudder is essential to reduce adverse yaw; however, it doesn't enhance the roll rate in the slightest. The stall is very Moth-like with similar speeds. The overall feeling is of an aerial barge as opposed to the light sailing dinghy of aircraft from the DH stable!

Displays in the Elf have to be a bit limited as to the range of manoeuvre – it's just a case of flying back and forth for the folks to see this unique aeroplane flying, while the commentator tells them all about it. The saving grace is that it looks pretty.

The circuit, approach and landing are flown at the same speeds as many of its contemporaries, and as long as we select 'stall' on the trimmers we can usually make a decent three-point arrival, which the soft undercarriage absorbs nicely. The Elf was not one of my favourite aeroplanes at the Collection, but neither was it over-demanding or difficult. It was just bland!

BA Swallow 2 G-AFCL – 1935

The Klemm Leichtflugzeugbau GmbH (Klemm Light Aircraft Company) was a German aircraft manufacturer noteworthy for sports and touring planes of the 1930s. The company had been founded by aircraft designer Dr Hans Klemm in 1926; Klemm had previously worked for both the Zeppelin Airship Company and Daimler Aircraft.

Klemm's L.25 model, which first flew in 1927, was aimed at the private pilot–owner looking for a not too expensive touring aircraft. To that end it was designed to be easy and docile to fly as well as economic to run. It was successful mainly due to its low wing loading, benign handling qualities and reliable engine. It was a tandem, two-seat monoplane with a low-slung 42ft span, broad chord wing. More than 600 L.25 models would be built and some were exported to Britain. In 1929 Klemm set up a UK agency and by 1933 twenty-seven L.25s had been imported and sold. Then the UK agent, Major E.F. Stephen, established the British Klemm Aeroplane Company to build the L.25 under licence. Some modifications followed, partly to ease production, and the French Salmson 75hp radial engine was replaced with a British seven-cylinder radial Pobjoy Cataract motor, giving 90hp. This was mounted uncowled in the nose with the off-centre propeller driven by a reduction gearbox. The twin exhaust pipes passed along the underside of the nose terminating just below the leading edge of the wing. This combination gave very smooth running and low noise. By 1935 the company had become the British Aircraft Manufacturing Company and the modified Klemm L.25 became the BA Swallow 2. One hundred and five Swallows were built by BAMC; roughly half of them were powered by the Blackburn Cirrus Minor four-cylinder inverted in-line engine.

Swallow G-AFCL is one of two known to be in flying condition and is finished in yellow and silver-grey. It was built in 1937 and has been in various private owners' hands since; it is still privately owned and in the care of the Collection. It looks like a powered glider but its neatly panelled fuselage gives it an air of sleekness. It is flown solo from the rear cockpit and the checks and starting procedures very much follow those of the Tomtit. Once running the engine is remarkably quiet; in fact from the cockpit, it is the slipstream that is a more prominent clue that it is going!

Taxying is easy; it has brakes, although over rough ground the long wings give the impression of a drunken sailor swaying from side to side. The take-off is a smooth, unhurried affair, which sets the tone for the rest of the flight. The Swallow is a slow-speed machine and the display is best flown showing off the big wings in serene and rather hushed flypasts. The circuit and landing is an equally unhurried event and the only challenge is getting the big bird to stop floating along and actually land!

13

Oddities

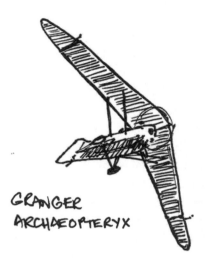

GRANGER
ARCHAEOPTERYX

During my time with the Shuttleworth Collection there were three aircraft that were running non-flyers, which were sometimes pulled out of the hangars and taxied around the crowd line for the public to be amazed by. They were:

The Granger Archaeopteryx
The Mignet Pou-du-Ciel 'Flying Flea'
Cierva C.30/Avro Rota Autogiro

I was fortunate enough to be allowed to taxi all of these wondrous machines around the airfield and in some ways I was thankful that I was not expected to fly them!

Granger Archaeopteryx G-ABXL – 1930

After the 1918 Armistice aerodynamic research continued into many aspects of aeronautics, with the search for increased stability and safety an important element. Pre-war work in this area by a brilliant Army officer called J.W. Dunne had conceived and built a series of swept-winged, tailless biplanes and monoplanes that flew very successfully. This led ex-RFC pilot Captain Geoffrey T.R. Hill MC, MSc, MIMechE, FRAeS, to explore a similar path to aerodynamic efficiency and safety. His tailless designs were also successful and in the 1920s and '30s he collaborated with Westland Aircraft in the production of several models of the aeroplane he called the Pterodactyl.

After seeing the success of the Pterodactyl, the two Granger brothers, who were Nottingham lace makers, decided to build their own aircraft in which to learn to fly. They designed a parasol swept-wing monoplane, with wingtip elevons and without a tailplane or elevator. Neither brother had any engineering training, which makes their handiwork all the more commendable. The construction of their aeroplane occupied three and a half years, the work being carried out under difficulties in a small garage.

The wing construction of the Archaeopteryx followed normal practice, with wooden spars and ribs covered with fabric. The fuselage was a wooden semi-monocoque with a length of only 14ft 10in, and the whole aircraft had a basic weight of 336lb. The arrangement of the wingtips was based on the Pterodactyl's, their movement being actuated by a control column with a part wheel on the top; normal rudder pedals were fitted.

The Archaeopteryx first flew at Hucknall near Nottingham in October 1930. Very interestingly, the aircraft was not initially registered with the Air Registration Board and flew without markings until two years later, on 3 June 1932, when it was given the registration G-ABXL. I find it hard to imagine that the regulators didn't get a bit peeved when they found out!

The brothers both piloted the aircraft many times and in June 1935 flew from Nottinghamshire to Hatfield in Hertfordshire for a flying display. Performance on the 32hp Bristol Cherub engine was marginal as long as the pilot weighed no more than 11st! The single Archaeopteryx built was flown regularly between 1930 and 1936 before being stored for thirty years at the Nottingham home of one of the brothers. The designers realised the type's significance as the forerunner of modern swept-wing aircraft, and on

28 April 1967, G–ABXL was presented to the Shuttleworth Collection by R.J.T. Granger, where it was restored to airworthy condition and flew again in June 1971 in the hands of John Lewis.

I remember seeing John flying the little blue bird before it was permanently grounded, because the Collection Trustees decided that some of its handling and stability issues could seriously jeopardise flight safety. Once airborne the Archaeopteryx seemed to fly remarkably well; however, performance was marginal and to get the machine to climb the pilot had to retract his elbows inside the already crowded tiny cockpit. The throttle is actually outside the cockpit, poking out of a slit in the linen! Although demonstrating normal longitudinal stability through most of the limited flight envelope, it was the interaction between the very short-coupled and rather rigidly sprung undercarriage and *terra firma* that brought the biggest problems. The result was, during both take-off and landing, a series of effectively uncontrollable kangaroo-like hops and bounces that had to be endured until either the aeroplane was airborne or the speed had dropped to a fast walking pace. This behaviour was perhaps the main reason for grounding the little beast!

During my time with Collection, the Granger brother's marvellous flying machine was regularly brought out and we taxied it around the flight line for folks to wonder at. The first trick was getting into it! The only way in was over the back of the canvas sling seat after a whole piece of the rear fuselage had been removed. Once aboard, that was replaced and fastened – an emergency exit was not an option! The fuel tank in the wing centre section feeds the engine by gravity and, once the engine is primed, the single ignition switch is selected on and the tiny two-bladed prop is twirled (it doesn't deserve the word 'swung') – in fact, it reminded me of someone starting a large model aircraft!

The Cherub then emits a most un-angelic holy racket. The two very short exhaust stubs on each side of the nose, emanating from the horizontally opposed cylinder heads, bark harshly for the duration. Once the engine is responding satisfactorily, the chocks are removed and about 1,500rpm will get the bird moving. The large rudder and pulses of power make it easy to manoeuvre on the ground, even in 10kt winds. Under way it is great fun to wheel this motorcycle of the air around. However, even at a fast walking speed any rough patches will give a hint of the uncomfortable pitching movement to the fuselage.

I would have loved to have been able to take up the challenge of flying this unique and unusual flying machine. However, having listened to John

Lewis's descriptions and read his report in David Ogilvy's excellent book *From Bleriot to Spitfire** I think that in this case discretion was the better part of valour. How those two lace-making brothers, who had no formal training in aircraft design and manufacture, got their creation to fly and taught themselves to fly it, I will never know. Hats off to you both, Messrs Granger!

Mignet HM.14 Pou-du-Ciel ('Flying Flea') G-AEBB

A French radio engineer called Henri Mignet had been designing, building and testing light or ultra-light aeroplanes since the early 1920s. Around 1930 he decided to design an aircraft that was suitable for the do-it-yourself home builder. He also decided that the design would be such as to eliminate the possibility of the amateur private pilot stalling or spinning, so making it very safe. He is reputed to have said that if anyone could construct a packing case and drive a car then they could build and fly his diminutive flying machine! In France the very common and easy to drive Model T Ford was known as the *Pou de la Route* – literally the 'louse of the road'. So Mignet decided that his new, radical design should be called the *Pou-du-Ciel* – literally the 'louse of the sky'; in English this became translated as the less prosaic and more alliterative 'Flying Flea'.

The HM.1 ' Flea followed a series of designs, and on 10 September 1933 Mignet piloted the first flight. In the following months, he made many test flights, totalling ten hours flying time, with progressive modifications to improve handling and performance. The prototype HM.14 had a wingspan of 20ft and was powered by a 17hp three-cylinder, two-stroke motorcycle engine. Subsequent examples were built with many optional engine and wingspan variations. In September 1934, the French aeronautical magazine *Les Ailes* (*Wings*) published an article by Mignet in which he described the HM.14. In November 1934, he published a book that gave all the dimensions, details of materials, plus descriptions and techniques, to enable readers to construct and fly their own HM.14s without further specialist help. In September 1935, the British Air League published an English translation of the article and it was also serialised in 1935 issues of the magazine *Newne's Practical Mechanics*.

---

* Airlife Publishing Ltd in 1991.

The HM.14 is most commonly described as a tandem-wing aircraft, without a horizontal tailplane. Construction of the airframe uses birch plywood sheet, spruce laths, steel tubing, steel cables, proprietary metal fittings, adhesives and linen fabric. Unlike conventional aircraft, the HM.14 has no ailerons or elevators, and no rudder pedals. The flight control system comprises simply of a conventional control stick. Fore-and-aft movement of the stick is transmitted via cables to the rear underside of the main wing, which is supported by a pylon-mounted pivot. Rearward movement of the stick increases the pitch and therefore the lift of the main wing and the aircraft will pitch up, forward stick movement has the reverse effect. Side-to-side movement of the stick controls the all-moving rudder (and a steerable tailwheel) and this produces a stable rolling motion due to the marked dihedral of both wings.

In late November 1934, Mignet exhibited his HM.14 at the Salon l'Aéronautique au Grand Palais in Paris, followed in early December by a public flying demonstration at Paris-Orly Airport. On 13 August 1935, Mignet crossed the English Channel from Saint-Inglevert to Lympne and on 17 August displayed the Flea to the press at Shoreham Airport. Earlier, on 14 July 1935, Stephen Appleby flew the first flight of his HM.14 (G-ADMH) at Heston Aerodrome, west of London. This was the first Flying Flea to fly in the UK and on 24 July 1935 the Air Ministry awarded it the first Authorisation to Fly document, equivalent to a UK Certificate of Airworthiness. By 1937 more than 6,000 copies of Mignet's handbook had been printed and nearly 100 Fleas had been UK registered. During 1936 and 1937 there were several fatal accidents following loss of control, which led the British Air League to recommend that further research should be completed. This was done in UK and France but public confidence in the *Pou-du-Ciel* was lost. Mignet continued to develop the tandem wing concept, but the aviation authorities in many countries withdrew the aircraft's certificates of airworthiness.

The Collection's Flying Flea was British-registered on 20 January 1936; however, little else is known about its pre-Second World War history. After the war it was with No. 124 Southampton Squadron of the Air Training Corps for many years. It donated G-AEBB to the Collection in 1967, after which it was restored to full running condition by Tony Dowson of the volunteer charitable organisation the Shuttleworth Veteran Aeroplane Society (SVAS). The SVAS is a collection of wonderful people who contribute in countless ways to the success of the Shuttleworth Collection and its aims.

The Flea is technically airworthy but, following the misfortunes of the late 1930s, the UK CAA does not allow it a Permit to Fly.

Like the Archaeopteryx, the Flea was regularly brought out for a public airing and, on a couple of occasions, I was invited to taxi it. Quite honestly I can remember little about the machine except that it was easier to get into than the Granger brothers' machine; although I did have to watch my head on the forward wing. Like the Archaeopteryx, the noise from the engine was deafening and the very peculiar and totally counterintuitive method of steering the tiny steerable tailwheel using the stick was very odd. I think I remember also that, like the Archaeopteryx, the throttle was outside the cockpit, but it was on the right. As I drove the little blue and silver machine around the crowd line I used to move the stick backwards and forwards so the folks might see the 20ft wing tilting around its hinge above my head.

Again there was always a strong urge to move out to the runway and break all the rules to see just how it flew. The *Pou-du-Ciel* was a revolutionary concept for its day and it is a great shame that there were hidden dangers in its unique design. I understand that today the Shuttleworth Flying Flea 'flies' suspended from the roof of one of the hangars at Old Warden.

Avro Rota G-AHMJ (K4234) – 1934

At the invitation of the UK Air Ministry, Spaniard Don Juan de la Cierva brought his first revolutionary (excuse the pun!) autogiro to Britain in 1925. This was the C.6A, which used an Avro 504 fuselage with the four-bladed rotor mounted on a pylon in place of the wings. A twin-seat version was developed and first flew in July 1926.

Unlike a helicopter, the rotor of an autogiro is not driven by mechanical means, such as the engine; instead the blades rely solely on forward speed for their rotation. Until the C.30A was developed, all the Cierva autogiros, and those built by other companies such as A. V. Roe and de Havilland, relied on conventional control surfaces on small wings and the empennage, operated in the usual way from the cockpit. The problem was that the power of these controls diminished with reducing speed. This was a major limitation on the aircraft's ability to fly slowly, which was its most advantageous characteristic. After further research and flight-testing, Cierva incorporated a pivoting rotor head that was controlled directly by the pilot, using a lever projecting down into the cockpit. Simple solutions are often the best! It also laid the foundation for the design of the helicopter.

The Avro Rota was a Cierva C.30A autogiro that was licence-built in the 1930s for military use by the RAF in the Army co-operation role. Twelve Rotas were produced by A.V. Roe and Co. Ltd in Manchester and were initially based at Old Sarum, near Salisbury in Wiltshire. They served throughout the Second World War with the RAF's only autogiro unit, No. 529 Squadron.

The Collection's Rota was built in 1934 and went directly into RAF service. Along with the other eleven Rotas it survived the war and was sold to Fairey Aviation in July 1946, where it helped in research and training for the Fairey Gyrodyne helicopter. However, in 1947 it was passed to the Hayes and Harlington Sea Cadets, where it stayed for seven years. In 1954 K4234 was transferred to the Collection, but it was many years before it was restored to exhibition condition by SVAS member Ken Hyde.

The Rota was another non–flying exhibit that escaped from the hangar at regular intervals for a runabout on the grass. At almost 20ft long, 11ft-high and with a rotor diameter of 37ft, the Rota was a sizeable, if not attractive, machine. Access to the cockpit was not easy, via a single step in the port side of the fuselage, co-ordinated use of a hand gripping the rear left pylon strut and a big swing of the right leg over the cockpit sill. The cockpit was very deep and basic instruments were fitted. The large 'stick' hanging down in the middle of the space between the pilot and the instrument panel was unnervingly odd. There were pedals on the floor that were only connected to the steerable tailwheel; there was no rudder at the back end, just a broad chord, fixed fin. At least the throttle was in the usual place on the left.

Starting the 140hp, Armstrong Siddeley Genet Major, seven-cylinder radial engine followed the procedures used for the similar Lynx in the Tutor. Once running and warmed up, the Rota needed quite a handful of power to get its 1,250lb weight moving. The blades drooped down at their ends and we usually restrained one of the three blades over the rear fuselage with a strop. The view ahead from the cockpit was very poor to non-existent, with the engine, pylon struts and undercarriage legs all getting in the way. As we taxied about close to the crowd but on the airfield side of the often unique and priceless Collection flying machines, the lack of a clear view ahead kept one on one's toes!

At one point, I think in the early 1990s, there was talk about the airworthiness of the Rota's rotor blades and whether we might be able to get it airborne again. As one of the few Collection pilots who had quite a lot of rotary wing experience, my ears pricked up at this possibility. However, it was discovered that the blades would need totally replacing, which was an expense too far, so I had to be satisfied with having a run around on the ground in this weird and wonderful machine.

14

Racers

MILES HAWK SPEED SIX

When I was a Collection pilot, Shuttleworth owned or had access to three air racers: the Miles Hawk Speed Six, the Percival Gull and the DH.88 Comet. In addition, Desmond Penrose kept his beautiful 1935 single-seat Percival Mew Gull (G-AEXF) at Old Warden. Of these, I flew the Gull and the Speed Six and came very close to flying the Comet (more of which later). I could have included the Gull in the chapter on tourers, as it was a touring aircraft, but it was also a very long-range racer (as was the Comet); moreover, the Gull also competed in several closed-circuit air races, so I include it here.

Miles Hawk Speed Six G-ADGP – 1935

The Hawk Major was designed by F.G. Miles, powered by a 130hp de Havilland Gipsy III engine and featured deep streamlined fairings around the undercarriage, quaintly known in the trade as 'trousers'! The prototype was first flown in 1934 and achieved second place in that year's King's Cup Race at an average speed of 147.78mph.

The aircraft sold well to private owners, including two that were fitted with smoke generators to allow them to be used as skywriters. An improved version (the M.2H) with flaps replaced the M.2F on the production line. A number of special one-off racing versions were also built. In October 1934, while competing in the MacRobertson Air Race, Squadron Leader M.C. McGregor flew a Hawk Major from RAF Mildenhall to Melbourne, Australia in seven days, fifteen hours. In 1936 Miles Hawk VI G-ADOD was entered in the Schlesinger Race from Portsmouth to Johannesburg and was flown by Flying Officer A.E. Clouston. He nearly made it all the way to Jo'burg but had to make a forced landing due to engine trouble 150 miles south of Salisbury, now Harare, Zimbabwe.*

A single-seat racing version of the Hawk Major was developed as the M.2L Hawk Speed Six with a 200hp de Havilland Gipsy Six engine; only three were ever built. After the war, one of these three, G-ADGP, known as 'No. 8' from its racing number on the rudder, was owned and raced for nearly eighteen years by renowned aircraft engineer and private pilot Ronald Paine. In 1971, 'No. 8' underwent a complete overhaul and refurbishment, after which Ron flew her to second place in the 1972 King's Cup Air Race. It remains in private hands and is lodged at the Collection for preservation in flying condition.

My first flight in the Speed Six was in June 1996 when I carried out its annual Permit to Fly air test. I subsequently displayed it twice. However, like many of the Collection's aeroplanes, once flown never forgotten. As I've said before, first impressions are often very telling and true – at least with aircraft they usually are! The Speed Six sits low to the ground, with a slightly hunched look, as if itching to go. The tiny cockpit canopy adds to its sleekness, as do its splendid 'trousers'. The rather handsome colour scheme is the original Miles design, with a gloss black fuselage and cream wings and tail. Looking around the aircraft gives the distinct impression that lots of TLC has been poured on this diminutive racer. It is 24ft long and the low, straight wings span 33ft. The fuel is contained in two tanks in each wing root, which

---

* Arthur Edmond Clouston, CB, DSO, DFC, AFC and bar (7 April 1908–1 January 1984) was a British test pilot and senior RAF officer who took part in several air races and record-breaking flights in the 1930s. He later commanded the ETPS and retired in 1960 with the rank of air commodore.

have external gauges à la Chipmunk. The Speed Six has split flaps that span about one third of each wing; the rest of the trailing edges are taken up with ailerons.

Access to the 'office' is via a short reinforced walkway on the right wing root and having squeezed carefully through the small aperture one gets an immediate sense of an aircraft built for a single purpose – to go as fast as possible on 200 horsepower! The cockpit is well instrumented and shows off the loving restoration efforts of the 1970s. The one slight oddity is the stick, which is a fairly short, slim metal rod with a basic grip at the top. The engine and tail trim levers fall readily to hand on the left, where the brake lever is also located. There is an additional long lever on the right that mechanically operates the flap, which can be either up or down.

The Speed Six has a battery and starter motor so, after the usual priming, the engine is started by pushing a button; when it catches there is no doubt – the 200 horses make themselves known in no uncertain fashion! Once all the checks are complete, taxying to the runway is relatively easy. Although the tailskid is fixed the differential brakes, set by a lever, again à la Chipmunk, are reasonably effective but small bursts of power are needed to reduce the radius of turn. The view ahead is restricted by the nose, but not as badly as in many taildraggers.

On take-off it is wise to set full throttle gradually so that the torque can be dealt with using progressive movement of the rudder pedals. The tail does not come up readily, a good push on the stick is necessary and the little aircraft gets into the air at around 55mph. It's a good idea to accelerate to 75mph in a very shallow climb, throttle the engine back from about 2,300rpm to 2,100 and then adjust the attitude to hold 80mph for the climb. This speed gives a good view over the nose and an ascent rate of about 1,200ft per minute. The most noticeable characteristic is the rather forward in-flight stick position and the apparent ineffectiveness of the tail trimmer to help hold it there.

Up and away this is an exciting little aeroplane. The very snug and small canopy (which I closed after take-off), the high cockpit sills above shoulder level and the eager acceleration gives the feeling of a fighter. However, that is dispelled by the very disappointing roll rates, even with full aileron and some balancing rudder applied. The Speed Six has a normal operating maximum speed of 221mph, which it can reach without difficulty. However, at that speed the stick is about as far forward as it will go and it is not possible to trim out the remaining push force of about 10lb. All this leads to an understanding that low-level displays will be more comfortable if the maximum speed used is limited to about 160mph. With an aircraft of its small size at 100–200ft that will still look fast.

At the other end of the speed range the stall speeds turn out to be 50mph with the flaps up and 45 with them down; the limiting speed for lowering flap is 65mph. This is not so much as a structural limit but because of the heaviness of the pull required on the lever. There was nothing to worry about with the behaviour of the aeroplane at the stall.

Displaying the Speed Six is fun: lots of low, fast flypasts, turns and wingovers as steep as one can manage and a low-speed flypast at 60mph with the flaps down. When ready to land it is best to fly downwind at 65mph or below so that the flaps can go down before the final turn. That part of the circuit can be a bit tricky, as the speed has to stay at 60 and the power has to come back to get the right descent path; letting the speed come back any further with bank on could get the little machine a bit close to the stall. Once lined up at a couple of hundred feet the speed can be reduced to 55 and the trimmer pulled well nose up, ready for the round-out and landing. The view is good until the very last few feet, when the nose starts to get in the way. I found that if the landing was mainwheels first the rather stiff undercarriage pitched the nose up and, despite the flap and low speed, the aircraft tended to float and then touch down tail first. Not disastrous, but not something that should be done too often in public view!

Overall, the experience of flying and displaying the Speed Six was yet another privilege that can only happen at the Shuttleworth Collection. To live, if only for a few minutes, in the shadow of all those great air racing pilots such as Alex Henshaw and Jim Mollinson is unforgettable.

Percival D.3 Gull G-ADPR – 1935

In 1932 a man with two first names, Edgar Percival, set up his own aviation design and manufacturing business – the Percival Aircraft Company. Percival was, by then, a well-known and respected aircraft designer and air racing pilot. Remarkably, by the age of 14 Australian-born Edgar had designed and flown two full-size gliders. In December 1915, at the age of 17, he volunteered for overseas service with the Australian Imperial Force (AIF). The following year he transferred from the AIF to pilot training with the

Royal Flying Corps. Once he had his wings, Percival was assigned to No. 60 Squadron in France, where his flying skills were praised by his CO. He also saw service in the Middle East and Greece. In 1918, while serving in Egypt, Percival designed his first powered aircraft, a special-purpose aircraft based on the Bristol F.2B, with a Rolls-Royce Eagle engine.

Following the First World War, Percival returned to Australia with three surplus aircraft, to do film work, stunt flying, barnstorming and charter flights. There he designed and built the winning entry in the 1924 Australian Aero Club light aircraft competition. In 1926, flying an aircraft that he had helped to design, he won a Federal Government challenge for both design and piloting skills.

Percival returned to England in 1929, where he was appointed as an Air Ministry test pilot. Percival was respected as a highly competitive and able air racing pilot, as well as being a rather fiery, impatient and irascible businessman and employer. During this period, Edgar Percival served in the RAF Reserve and was a founding member of the Guild of Air Pilots and Air Navigators. He became known as 'The Hat' because, much like Igor Sikorsky, he usually flew wearing a natty trilby!

In 1932, he began searching for an established manufacturer to produce a light aeroplane that he had designed, which he called the Percival Gull. Finding no company willing and able to take on production, Percival initiated the Percival Aircraft Company. Running the business from his private address in London, Percival then arranged for series production to be contracted out to the aforementioned George Parnall & Sons. In 1934, after twenty-four Gulls had been produced at Parnall's, Percival set up his own factory at London Gravesend Airport, Kent.

Edgar Percival's aircraft were renowned for their graceful lines and outstanding performance. As a test pilot, Percival continued to fly his own creations; in 1935, he flew a Gull from England to Morocco and back in one day, the first pilot ever to do so. In 1933, another Australian, Charles Kingsford-Smith, flew a Percival Gull IV from England to Australia in the record-breaking time of seven days, four hours and forty-four minutes.

The Gull went through many changes and the Collection's 1935 Gull, G-ADPR, was the ultimate version: the D.3 Gull Six. It was fitted with a 200hp DH Gipsy Six, six-cylinder, in-line engine. This Gull had the same length and wingspan as earlier variants, but was 195lb heavier and, with a top speed of 178mph, was much faster. This airframe had belonged to the famous 1930s New Zealand aviatrix Jean Batten. She made at least two memorable record-breaking flights in G-ADPR. On 11 November 1935, she departed Lympne in southern England and flew two legs to Senegal, West Africa. After a twelve-and-a-half-hour Atlantic crossing on 13 November, she arrived at Port Natal, Brazil. For this amazing achievement Batten was awarded the Britannia Trophy. On 5 October 1936, she flew from Lympne to Darwin in the record time of five days, twenty-one hours, three minutes, then flying on across the Tasman Sea to Auckland to set another total record time of eleven days, forty-five minutes.

On 25 April 1961 G-ADPR was passed to the Collection by the Percival Aircraft Company, in a non-flying state. It was rebuilt in the late 1980s and first flew from Old Warden in July 1991. On that day I flew the Magister for airborne photography with the late Angus McVitie at the controls of the Gull. In 1996 the Gull was air-freighted back to New Zealand and it flew over Auckland to mark the sixtieth anniversary of Jean Batten's record-breaking flight. The aeroplane now graces the Auckland International Airport terminal.

I first flew the Gull on 20 April 1994 and displayed it three times after that. It is a very attractive, but simultaneously purposeful-looking aircraft and the overall silver finish really shines on a summer's day. It's one of those aircraft that looks right, so probably flies right. Walking round it one can't help noticing the various transfers applied to the nose and the tail. The latter mark the various record-breaking destinations and those on the nose show that sponsorship is nothing new – Wakefield Patent Castrol Motor Oil being prominent!

The enclosed cabin is laid out so that the pilot sits in the middle with two passenger seats behind. There's plenty of room and the Gull is well equipped with a full suite of flight and engine instruments, flaps, brakes and not too bad a view around the nose on the ground. When the Gipsy 6 starts you know it! The short exhaust stubs under the nose emit a harsh, continuous, bark. Taxying is relatively easy, once you get used to the rather sharp-acting wheel brakes. The Gull is equipped with a castoring tailwheel so manoeuvring is also easy and effective. The take-off is made without flaps and is quite brisk. During a display from the north-easterly runway at Old Warden it was feasible to get airborne early enough to take the Gull 'around the bend' at about 120mph directly from take-off.

Up and away there are no surprises. The Gull is a well-designed aeroplane with good stability and control characteristics. The stall occurs at a surprisingly low speed for an aircraft of its size and weight (about 50mph with the flaps up and 45 with flaps down) and is generally well-behaved. With 200 horses up front the recovery is rapid, but you do have to be ready with the rudder to counteract the prominent torque and slipstream effects. Cruising at 150mph is easily possible and the VNE of 178mph can be reached in a shallow dive. The controls do, naturally, get heavier at the higher speeds, especially the ailerons, but there seemed to be no stability issues.

The Gull was a delight to display, even though aerobatics were not permitted. Low fast flypasts at 150mph and steep turns and wingovers in a blue sky looked good and were usually much appreciated. The only thing that preyed upon my mind, especially if there was not much headwind to land into, was stopping. The approach speed was an initial 80mph, reducing to 70 with flap down and no less than 60 over the end of the runway. It was important to aim to touch down as soon as possible because the Gull had a good deal of inertia and the brakes were very sensitive. In fact, there were occasions when even with the spade grip stick fully back the tail started to lift under braking, so I had to ease off. I never actually ran out of runway but on one hot, still August day came close to it!

It was and is a great privilege to have flown such a famous flying machine; and to have sat where Jean Batten sat, for so many hours. Also to marvel at the genius of the man with the hat and two first names, all the while enjoying his immaculate design.

De Havilland DH.88 Comet G-ACSS – 1934

One day, in early 1994, Roger 'Dodge' Bailey and I were summoned into the considerable presence of the chief pilot, John Lewis. He told us that the operations folk and aviation trustee had decided that we were going to be the next DH.88 Comet pilots. At that time the Comet was being operated out of the BAe airfield at Hatfield, 30 miles south of Old Warden. Hatfield had been the centre of manufacture and flight testing for all DH aircraft since 1933. The reason for this *modus operandi* was that the runway at Old Warden was of insufficient length for safe Comet operations. I had already flown the DH Comet, but that was the DH.106 jet airliner model, not the much earlier DH.88 air racing version!

The de Havilland DH.88 Comet is a two-seat, twin-engined aircraft that was designed specifically to participate in the 1934 England–Australia

Blackburn B-2. (Steven Jefferson)

DH Cirrus Moth G-EBWD. (Steven Jefferson)

DH Hornet Moth. (Steven Jefferson)

Bristol Boxkite. (Steven Jefferson)

Avro Triplane. (Steven Jefferson)

Bristol Fighter. (Steven Jefferson)

Jean Batten's Percival Gull. (Steven Jefferson)

Hawker Tomtit. (Steven Jefferson)

Gordon McClymont on his first flight in the Avro Tutor. Photographed by Steven Jefferson from the Shuttleworth Collection's Tiger Moth, flown by the author. (Steven Jefferson)

Parnell Elf. (Steven Jefferson)

Hucks Starter with Hind. (Steven Jefferson)

The author's first take-off in Spitfire Vc AR501. (Steven Jefferson)

Supermarine Spitfire Vc AR501 on display. (Steven Jefferson)

The Harvard Formation Team. (Author's collection)

Jet Heritage Hunter T.7 G–BOOM leading single-seat Hunter G–HUNT. (PRM Aviation Collection)

Jet Heritage Jet Provost pair. (Peter R. March)

MacRobertson Air Race from the United Kingdom to Australia. The race was devised by the Lord Mayor of Melbourne, and a prize fund of $75,000 was put up by Sir Macpherson Robertson, a wealthy Australian confectionery manufacturer, on the condition that the race be named after his MacRobertson company. The race was organised by the British Royal Aero Club, and would run from RAF Mildenhall in East Anglia to Flemington Racecourse, Melbourne, a distance of 11,300 miles (18,200km). A total of twenty-seven stops were provided with stocks of fuel and oil by Shell and Stanavo. The Royal Aero Club put some effort into persuading the countries along the route to improve the facilities at the stopping points.

The basic rules were:

No limit to the size of aircraft or power; no limit to crew size
No pilot was to join the aircraft after it left England
All aircraft had to carry three days' rations per crew member, floats, smoke signals and efficient instruments.

There were prizes for the outright fastest aircraft, and for the best performance on a handicap formula by any aircraft finishing within sixteen days. Take-off was set at dawn (6.30 a.m.), on Saturday, 20 October 1934.

Development of the Comet was initiated by Geoffrey de Havilland, along with the support of the DH board, which was keen for the prestige that would come from producing the victorious aircraft, as well as any gain from the research involved in producing it. The Comet was designed by A.E. Hagg around the specific requirements of the race. The innovative design was a stressed-skin, twin-engined, cantilever monoplane, complete with an enclosed cockpit, retractable undercarriage, landing flaps, and variable-pitch propellers.

The Comet racer had a tapered, high aspect ratio wing and was powered by two Gipsy Six R engines, a specially tuned version of the Gipsy Six. Construction was almost entirely of wood, lightweight magnesium–aluminium alloy being confined to high-stress components such as the engine bearers and undercarriage, and to complex curved fairings such as the engine cowlings and wing root fairings. Manually operated split flaps were fitted below the wing inboard trailing edges and the lower fuselage. The rudder and elevators fitted to the conventional tail had horn mass balances. Aerodynamic efficiency was the design priority and it was therefore decided to use a thin wing of RAF34 section.

The fuselage was built principally from plywood over spruce longerons. To achieve the necessary compound curves, the upper and lower forward sections were built up from spruce planking. As with the wing, the strength of the structure was dependent upon the skin. Fuel was carried in three fuselage tanks: two main tanks in the nose and centre section. A third auxiliary tank, of only 20-gallon capacity, was placed immediately behind and could be used to adjust the aircraft's trim. The pilot and navigator were seated in tandem in a cockpit set aft of the wing. While dual flight controls were fitted, only the forward cockpit had a full set of flight instruments. The main undercarriage retracted backwards into the engine nacelles and was operated manually, requiring fourteen turns of a large hand-wheel located on the right-hand side of the cockpit.

A total of three Comets were produced for the race, all for private owners at the discounted price of £5,000 per aircraft. The aircraft underwent a rapid development cycle, performing its maiden flight only six weeks prior to the race. Mr A.O. Edwards purchased G-ACSS and had it painted all-over red and named after the Grosvenor House Hotel, which he managed. He engaged C.W.A. Scott and Tom Campbell-Black to fly it in the race.

After a very eventful flight they crossed the finishing line at 3.33 p.m. (local time) on Monday, 23 October. Their official time was seventy-one hours eighteen seconds and they emerged as the winner. Two further examples of the DH.88 were later built. The Comet went on to establish a multitude of aviation records, both during the race and in its aftermath, as well as participating in many further races. Several examples were bought and evaluated by national governments, typically as mail planes.

Prior to 1994 George Ellis had been the main pilot for the Comet, with Angus McVitie as reserve. George was about to leave the UK and Angus was about to retire, hence the need to find two other pilots. John told Dodge and I that we would need to start studying all the paperwork, go to Hatfield and arrange to practise operating the undercarriage (with the aircraft on jacks) and flaps, starting the engines, taxying it and generally getting very familiar with all its systems before we would start flying. So we set the wheels in motion.

However, not many weeks later, while the aircraft was being readied for a season's flying, we were told that it was all going to change. This was getting very like government flight testing! It transpired that BAe, during yet another of its rationalisations and impending name changes, had decided that all flight operations from Hatfield would cease and that the airfield would be sold off for development. The Comet now had to be flown from elsewhere or disassembled and brought back to Old Warden. In the event, following the closure of Hatfield in 1994, the aircraft returned to Old Warden where, of course, the runway was still too short to allow safe operation. The runway was lengthened by 1999 but then, in 2002, the Comet suffered undercarriage failure when landing after its first test flight and research showed that as originally designed the legs were liable to failure under certain conditions.

Subsequently, modifications to the structure were approved and implemented, and the aircraft flew again in the very capable hands of Dodge Bailey. Everything comes to he who waits! After successful test flights on 1 August 2014 it is now a regular performer at Shuttleworth air displays. Meanwhile, back at the ranch in 1994 the Comet arrived in bits, was put back together and was wheeled out for us to taxi for the crowds to see. I was privileged to do this on several occasions.

Getting aboard is fairly straightforward via the wing walkway and under the side-folding canopy that covers both seats. The front seat is comfortable, as it had to be for those three-day flights! Starting the engines using electrical power is virtually the same as starting the Gipsy 6 in the Hawk Speed Six and their raw power is very evident. The most noticeable feature of the Comet on the ground is the appalling view ahead. The seating position is well aft of the wing leading edge, so the fuselage ahead of the pilot, including the nose that contains most of the fuel, gets very much in the way and the engines obstruct the view to each side. Thankfully the brakes and castoring tailwheel, as well as the ability to use asymmetric power, all make turning the aeroplane easy – so helping to avoid very embarrassing and expensive contact with other aircraft and people on the flight line.

While taxying the challenges of landing this sleek beast were all too apparent. The thin, highly tapered wings with pointy ends could easily cause a sharp wing-drop at or near the stall. Moreover, the lack of any view of the runway below several hundred feet would mitigate against going for a long straight-in approach path or any attempt at a tail down or three-point landing. As noted above, Dodge Bailey did get to fly the Comet eventually, nearly twenty years after we were first asked to prepare for it! He, like me, can only doff his aviator's helmet at those aviators who flew this machine all those years ago, men who had to operate from airfields across the world and land in all sorts of conditions. Well done, gentlemen – I only wish I could have joined you!

15

Fighting Biplanes

Hawker Hind G-AENP (K5414)

In 1926, the Air Ministry put out a requirement for a metal-framed, two-seat, high-performance light bomber, with a maximum speed of 160mph. Designs were tendered by Hawker, Avro, de Havilland and Fairey. Hawker's winning design was a single-bay biplane powered by a Rolls-Royce Kestrel, water-cooled V12 engine. It had, as the specification required, a metal structure covered by aluminium panels and fabric. The crew of two sat in tandem cockpits, with the pilot sitting under the wing trailing edge, and operating a single .303in Vickers machine gun mounted on the port side of the cockpit. The observer sat behind the pilot, and was armed with a single Lewis gun on a ring mount. Up to 520lb (240kg) of bombs could be carried under the aircraft's wings. The prototype was named the Hart, an old term used for a stag; it first flew in June 1928 and demonstrated good performance and handling. It achieved 176mph in level flight and 282mph in a dive.

The Hart was the first of a long line of Hawker biplanes that dominated many roles in the 1930s' RAF; other variants followed, with names such as Audax, Fury, Demon and Nimrod. The Hind was the ultimate land-based development of the line and poetically closed the circle with a name of a deer, this time a female.

The Hind differed from its many predecessors in having a 640hp version of the RR Kestrel, a tailwheel and a cutaway rear cockpit to provide more scope for the gunner. It first flew in September 1934 and entered RAF service a year later. More than 500 Hinds were produced; they replaced most in-service Harts and many were operated by several overseas air forces.

The Collection's Hind was one of a batch of twenty delivered to the Afghan Air Force in 1938. In 1968 one of these was offered to the RAF Museum and a second to the Shuttleworth Collection. The RAF Museum example was collected by RAF Hercules, but the retrieval of the Collection's specimen was only made possible through the initiative of Bill Collard, an SVAS member, who persuaded the senior management of the Ford Motor Company (where he was also a manager) to use the 6,000-mile journey as a pre-service trial for a new Ford truck. With the considerable help of Vernon Maitland of Excelsior Coaches the retrieval was completed successfully in 1971. After a ten-year restoration programme the Hind was flown again, in Afghan colours, by Dickie Martin on 17 August 1981. It was later repainted in 15 Squadron RAF colours and given the military serial K5414.

The Hind had long been in my sights as one I must fly. My friend and fellow Shuttleworth pilot, Stu Waring, was already flying it when he gave me my first cockpit tour and hints and tips on how to operate it. However, it would be many months before 'management' decided that I was up to handling the Hind in the air.

It is an attractive and impressive-looking aeroplane that gives off an air of sleek purposefulness. It is tall and has a sophisticated, if not aloof, air as it awaits whichever bold young man is going to stride up and try to tame it! Walking round before flight it is essential to check some additional items to the usual general condition aspects. The engine radiator is below the centre section of the wing, between the undercarriage legs, and is extended and retracted to control the temperature of the coolant; so that, and the adjacent oil cooler matrices, must be checked for blockages by grass or debris, as well as looking for leaks. The other, rather odd, item to check is the assembly of circular weights bolted to a bar running athwartships, halfway between the cockpits and the tail. These must be fitted and secure if the Hind is being flown solo, otherwise the centre of gravity could be too far forward for safe flight.

Climbing up the shiny, silver fuselage into the cockpit is the usual challenge of setting off with the correct foot. Two very useful handholds on the trailing edge of the wing help when descending onto the seat. The cockpit is large and some of the lesser-used knobs and levers lie at the extremes of comfortable reach. The instrument panel is furnished, somewhat randomly, with all the usual flight and engine instruments, and looking down there is no floor as such. So anything that is dropped is likely to lie in the bottom of the fuselage until retrieved with difficulty. I remember, from sitting in one, that this was also a feature of the Hurricane, a descendant of the Hind.

Now comes another novel event. The Hind is best started by the Collection's Hucks Starter; named after its inventor Bentfield Hucks. This original 1920s machine is mounted on and driven by a power take-off of a Model T Ford truck. The rather Heath Robinson device is driven up to the nose of the aircraft and the driveshaft is linked to a coupling in the propeller spinner. Once the engine priming is finished and the magnetos selected on, the signal is given and the Hucks operator engages the drive, the aeroplane lurches in response, the prop turns until the engine fires and then the starter automatically disengages.* Thereafter it is a case of getting the Kestrel to run smoothly at about 1,100rpm, avoiding a couple of bands where some rough running can occur. Once the fuel and oil pressures have stabilised it is time to think about controlling the coolant temperature. It is now that the large wheel on the lower right and the big curved indicator beneath the instrument panel come into their own; both are reminiscent of something from a submarine – not an elegant aeroplane such as the Hind! The wheel is turned, with not a little effort, to extend or retract the radiator and the indicator shows how far out it is. The ideal temperature is 75–85°C. We soon learned that at least half-open is right for a summer's day!

With its well-sprung and damped undercarriage, castoring tailwheel and pneumatic brakes the Hind is easy to move around the airfield. The brakes are operated by air pressure from an on-board bottle, which is charged before flight. Hence, we were warned to avoid too much activity on the rudder pedals with brake applied (via a lever on the control column) as the pressure might fall to zero before the aircraft was back on the chocks. As usual there is no view directly ahead, so weaving is necessary. Once the magneto

---

* If the Hucks is not available a hand-cranked starter handle can be used.

and pre-take-off checks have been completed the take-off is a smooth and quick affair, even with the very moderate +1½psi boost used to preserve the motor. We are flying at 55mph after a ground roll of only 200 yards. The Hind accelerates easily to 100mph and, at that speed, will climb at around 1,200ft per minute.

The Kestrel, which is a predecessor to the bigger Merlin, emits a soft growl and is easy to control. Cruising at 150mph, with the boost set at +1psi and 2,300rpm (the maximum is +3½ and 2,900) is a very pleasant experience. The muffled sound of the engine, the wind singing through the wires and the solid, stable feel of this elegant aeroplane all add to a heightened sense of well-being and professional satisfaction. I reflect that I was right to look forward to flying the Hind. Before practising some display moves, I need to stall it. After checking all the engine parameters and a taking a good look around the sky, I smoothly close the throttle. It goes very quiet and the speed drops quite quickly. At about 50mph the faultless handling becomes much less assured, a distinct sense of the approaching stall is felt at about 45 and the nose drops gently at about 43mph. There is no difficulty in keeping the Hind in balance, as the rudder is still effective and the wings stay level without correction. However, one feature is that there is a bit of aileron snatch just as the stall occurs; nothing alarming but it spurs me into thinking that I shouldn't hold off too long on landing.

By now a less likeable feature of the Hind is beginning to bother me. Ever since take-off the temperature in the cockpit has risen steadily. Perhaps the hot air coming out of the radiator beneath my feet is being drawn up through the floor? Whatever it is, I make a mental note not to overdress for a summer display slot. Talking of which, I try out some steep turns, wingovers and a barrel roll.** The Hind's handling was good in pitch and yaw but the roll rates were only moderate and the aileron forces were fairly high. The other factor that would come into play during a display was the poor view into the turn because of the upper wing getting in the way. Nevertheless, a spirited display would be possible to show off the Hind's beautiful lines and good performance.

Back in the circuit the Hind once more shows its pedigree and landing turns out to be relatively easy. However, nobody told me about the 'flat spot' that occurs at about 65mph and at about 100ft on the final approach.

** This was before the CAA reviewed the Permits to Fly, which stopped aerobatics in nearly all the Collection's aircraft.

At this point the light exhaust noise from the Kestrel stops momentarily and the prop appears to pause. Just as the adrenalin kicks in, things return to normal. Phew! It's something to do with mixture, low rpm and speed. Even when I knew about it, I found that it never failed to give me a fizz of anxiety just before landing. Once on the ground the Hind does tend to wander directionally and it is important to be alert and ready with the rudder and brakes.

I displayed the Hind at Old Warden and at Duxford; it was always an enormous pleasure and privilege. Taking off at Old Warden on the north-easterly runway, holding it down to 100ft and turning at 60 degrees of bank round the bend in the display line was a great way to start. With all that speed and even with moderate power settings, steep climbs, wingovers and swoops back down the line were easily and safely flown. Although I had done a barrel roll up and away I never did do aerobatics during a display; somehow it just didn't seem appropriate. On the 1993 August Bank Holiday weekend I displayed three Hawker products in three days: the Hunter at RAF Valley in North Wales and the Hind and the Tomtit at Old Warden. Never mind 'Aaah, de Havilland!' – more 'Oooh, Hawker!'

Gloster Gladiator G-AMRK (L8032) – 1935

In 1930, the Air Ministry issued Specification F7/30, which sought an air-craft capable of a maximum speed of at least 250mph, with armament of four machine guns and handling good enough for the fighter to be used by both day and night squadrons.

The Gloster Aircraft Company recognised that, instead of developing an all-new design from scratch, its Gauntlet fighter could be used as a basis for a contender to meet Specification F7/30. Thus development of what would become the Gladiator began as a private venture, internally designated as the SS.37. The design team was led by H.P. Folland, who had designed *inter alia*, the S.E.5. Folland soon made changes to improve the aircraft's suitability to meet the specification. The wing design adopted single-bay wings, instead of the two-bay wings of the Gauntlet, and two pairs of interplane struts were also removed to reduce drag. The Bristol Mercury ME 30 radial engine, capable of generating 700hp, was selected to power the SS.37, and a very neat cantilever main undercarriage was fitted, which incorporated Dowty internally sprung wheel struts.

On 12 September 1934, the SS.37 prototype made its first flight, piloted by Gloster chief test pilot Gerry Sayer. On 3 April 1935, the prototype was transferred to the RAF, receiving the serial K5200, and commenced operational evaluations. Around the same time, Gloster went ahead with a further improved version, featuring an 840hp Mercury IX engine, a two-bladed, wooden, fixed-pitch propeller, improved wheel disks and a fully enclosed cockpit with a sliding hood. In June 1935, the British government mandated an urgent expansion of the RAF to counter emerging threats to peace, which culminated in an initial order for twenty-three aircraft. On 1 July 1935, the aircraft formally received the name Gladiator.

The Gladiator Mk I was delivered to the RAF from July 1936, becoming operational in January 1937. The Gladiator was to be the last British biplane fighter to be manufactured and the first to feature an enclosed cockpit. It possessed a top speed of about 257mph yet, even as the Gladiator was introduced, it was already being eclipsed by new-generation monoplane fighters, such as the Hawker Hurricane, Supermarine Spitfire and the Messerschmitt Bf 109. A total of 747 aircraft were built (483 RAF, 98 RN); 216 were exported to thirteen countries, some of these were from the total allotted to the RAF.

The Collection's example was the last production Gladiator I. It was built in 1937 but not actually assembled until 1938. In 1948 it, together with Gladiator II N5903, was bought by Glosters. In 1950 the two were delivered to Air Service Training for use as instructional airframes at Hamble and Ansty. When Ansty closed the aircraft were bought by ex-Fleet Air Arm pilot Viv Bellamy for a nominal sum. L8032 was restored and flew again as G-AMRK and, in 1953, it was bought back by Glosters. In 1956, L8032 was returned to full military specification in 72 Squadron markings, albeit with the fictitious serial K8032. When Gloster Aircraft closed in 1960 the Gladiator was presented to the Collection for safekeeping. In 1990 the aircraft was repainted in a camouflage scheme with No. 247 Squadron codes and it wore these until a fabric recover was carried out in 1996. When finished, the Gladiator emerged in Norwegian colours for filming. In 2007 it re-appeared as K7985 of 73 Squadron RAF, the aircraft flown by the Second World War Ace 'Cobber' Kain at the 1937 Hendon Air Pageant.

I don't mind admitting that I was a little intimidated while preparing myself to fly the 'Glad'. By now I had been told at length about the vagaries of the Mercury engine in its uncertain response to rapid applications of throttle; as well as the Glad's tendency to ground loop after landing. I had actually seen the result of a Mercury throttle mishandling when, on 21 June 1987 at a display at Denham airfield, I watched in horror as John Romain's painstaking and lengthy rebuild of a Bristol Blenheim all came to nought when it crashed. The accident was caused by the pilot (not John) carrying out a poorly executed touch and go landing, during which he applied power too quickly and caused one engine to suffer a rich mixture cut, while the other ran up to full power. The resulting loss of directional control caused the newly rebuilt Blenheim to cartwheel off the runway. Amazingly the three occupants survived and, even more amazingly, John rebuilt it again and it flies on the display circuit to this day. I had also witnessed one of the Collection pilots ground loop the Gladiator after landing, which damaged the undercarriage.

Hence, with some trepidation, tinged with excitement and a sense of history, I walked up to the big biplane. The dominating feature is the aforesaid big, round Mercury motor, surrounded by its large cowling. With much of the aircraft out of reach and very few wires on show, the external check is more of a 'once over' done in admiration of the Glad's solid and rather hefty lines. Arriving back at the wing trailing edge, I stepped up onto the small reinforced panel on the wing root below the cockpit. Trying hard to keep my balance and not put a foot through the wing fabric, I climbed over the open side panel into the cockpit, slid down into the seat and strapped in. Now I received the first of the pleasant surprises still to come. Compared with the Hind, this cockpit is well organised and looks relatively modern. The standard six instruments occupied the centre of the instrument panel in very orderly fashion. The other engine and associated dials were neatly arranged around it and the various levers and switches were mostly where I expected to find them. I adjusted the rudder pedals rearwards with the star-shaped wheel in the middle of the bar using my foot; the last occupant must have been one of the bigger guys!

I did a full check around the cockpit, including a full and free movement test of the flying controls using the spade-gripped stick and put the brakes on. Outside, the trolley-acc (a mobile battery pack), had been wheeled up alongside and plugged in. With the 'ground/flight' switch at 'ground', the electricity can start the engine. I cracked the throttle open by a small amount, made sure that the ignition switches were off and called out 'Ready to prime'. Using the priming knob on the right I gave the Mercury about four full shots of petrol and left about half a stroke ready to catch the engine when it fired. Now I called 'Ready for starting'. With the stick held fully back and magneto switches on, I pressed the starter switch and waited for the engine to fire. The big prop turned over apparently quite lazily for a couple of turns and then noise and smoke announced that the Mercury had come alive. Having made sure that the 'starter engaged' warning light was out, I turned the starter magneto off, screwed down the priming pump and turned its selector cock off. A check round of the engine instruments and fuel pressure completed the checklist, so I put the 'ground/flight' switch to 'flight' and waved the trolley-acc away.

The Mercury idles quite smoothly at the astonishingly low rpm of 600 and when it was warmed up a man was despatched to the tail end to drape his body over the rear fuselage while I set 1,800rpm and zero boost to check that the magneto drops were less than 120rpm. Another drawback of the Bristol Mercury is its propensity to carburettor icing, even on nice summer days. So after the magneto check I operated the air shutter control to make sure that in 'hot' there was a perceptible drop in rpm. If there was, then there was nothing left that would stop us aviating today in Mr Gloster's excellent flying machine.

Taxying the Glad is very easy, it has good brakes and well-damped under-carriage. The hood stayed slid fully back so that I could lean out as I weaved along to see that the way ahead wasn't previously occupied. Having the large, round cowling attached to the nose means that the view is even more hampered than with the slimmer-nosed, in-line-engined aeroplanes. Being a more sophisticated machine, the Gladiator's pre-take-off checklist is quite a bit longer than some of its predecessors. The hood is locked open, side panels are closed and harness locked, the elevator trim is set to zero and the flaps are up. Fuel selection and pressure, air shutter open, mixture and oil cooler set to normal all precede the usual final check of the flight instruments and flying controls. We're ready to go!

Because the Mercury is a large rotating mass, we have to be aware that it will cause gyroscopic forces if we move the aeroplane too rapidly in pitch. So on take-off I opened the throttle progressively and I raised the tail slowly and not too far. Even with only +1psi boost applied at max rpm the aircraft accelerated well and lifted off at 55–60mph, accelerated quickly to 95mph and climbed at more than 2,000ft per minute – unheard of performance for a Shuttleworth aeroplane!

At 5,000ft, reached in only a couple of minutes, with 2,200rpm and zero boost the Glad slips along at just less than 150mph; this will give a fuel consumption of 35 gallons per hour. With a fuel load of 83 gallons this will allow just over two hours of safe flight. However, when the machine was at war this time would have reduced markedly and allowed about an hour's combat at 20,000ft. With the hood closed, which I did just after take-off, the sensation is of smooth powerful flight. The engine's muffled constant growl and lack of a wild draught around my head could become quite soporific. However, it was time to put this machine through its paces. I had already noted that the Glad possessed the sort of handling qualities and light but positive stability that must have marked it out as a good air-to-air fighter. Especially nice was the quick rate of roll with crisp lateral response and relatively light control forces. I felt confident enough to try a few aerobatics, looping from 160mph, attainable in level flight with 2,400rpm and +1psi boost, and rolling at 140mph, but avoiding negative G, which would cause the engine to cut out momentarily. Steep turns and wingovers were delightfully easy, although, as usual in a biplane, the view into the turn was hampered by the upper wing.

Slowing down and holding level flight brought about a well-behaved stall at just under 50mph, with no pre-stall buffeting. Now was the time to try operating the flaps. Once selected down they are pumped into position with a large handle on the left of the seat. It was more effective than I had expected and all four flaps were down in about ten seconds, after a dozen or so strokes of the handle. It was easy to check the upper flap positions visually and there was only a slight nose-down trim change and no noticeable reduction in the stalling speed.

Now it was time to go back to Old Warden for a couple of circuits. I descended at low power and made sure that the air shutter was closed to get heat to the carburettor. Once in the circuit and below the limiting speed of 78mph, I lowered the flaps and set up for a landing. Having slid back the hood and locked it open, checked the fuel, air shutter and mixture, I turned onto a gentle finals turn aiming for a shallow approach angle to avoid throttling back too far and rolled out at 300ft with about 65mph. Now my view of the airfield was hindered by the nose but, using peripheral cues, I continued the descent, letting the speed trickle back to 55mph over the end of the strip. At this point I throttled right back and reminded myself that, should I have to go around, I must make the throttle movement slow and progressive. As it was, the attitude came nicely up to a three-pointer and the big fighter settled down nicely. There was a little bounce on a couple of bumps in the grass but we just rode over those. Now it was just a case of not relaxing until we had virtually stopped, staying alert to any tendency to swing and being ready with the rudder and brakes to counter it.

The Gladiator is one of those aeroplanes that gets rapidly under one's skin. It's not as pretty as the Hind, not as famous as the Spitfire, but it is one of the finest-handling aircraft that I have flown. I let it down only once, literally. At a display day at Old Warden with easterly winds we were using the appropriate runway. This was the least-favoured by all the pilots as it had a downhill gradient and the approach was over trees and adjacent to the No. 1 Hangar and public entrance gate. I had finished my display and turned downwind a bit too early, so leaving myself not a lot of sky in which to slow down, lower the flaps and get everything properly set up. That meant that I rushed things and turned in a bit on the high side and too close in. I throttled back as much as I dare and stuck the nose down to reduce height, but not exceed the 78mph flap-limiting speed. Then I was suddenly aware of the trees looming closer beneath me. This was simultaneous with a bout of tree-generated turbulence. It was at this point that I made the wrong decision: I elected to continue the approach. As the old saying goes 'a bad approach usually means a bad landing'. In this case I overcompensated for getting a bit low and ended up clearing the trees too high to land on the first part of the strip. That meant that I would end up floating downhill looking for the ground and picking up speed. I took all the power off and made the fundamental error of trying to land too soon. It all resolved itself in an enormous bounce. Being acutely aware of the danger of opening the throttle too rapidly, I just held the three-point attitude and waited for the ground to come up and hit me. Which it did without ceremony. Thankfully the speed was now so low that the Glad stayed down. I stopped, turned gingerly back towards the flight line and crept red-faced back to my parking spot. Nothing was said officially, the undercarriage was checked and found undamaged, but there was some banter from the boys to be endured – deservedly so!

The Gladiator is an absolute delight to fly. In displays it was possible to go straight into a very steep climb and wingover, or even half Cuban, to turn around for the first pass, which can be made at 100ft and close to 200mph without difficulty. The steep turns, either at crowd centre or around the bend, can be made safely with 60 degrees of bank, and showing off the quick rates of roll and rapid climbs is a great joy. No wonder the Gladiator is such a crowd-pleaser. I took it to Duxford for one of the big Flying Legends displays. Sadly that was more than ten years before Stephen Grey's Fighter Collection had restored and flown its Gladiator II, G-GLAD. That was originally N5903, the 'sister' of L8032, which was bought by Glosters in 1948 – sixty years before it would once more get air under its wheels at Duxford in the very capable hands of Peter Kynsey. I am so 'glad' that I joined the band of 'Glad' pilots, albeit late in my career!

16

Supermarine Spitfire

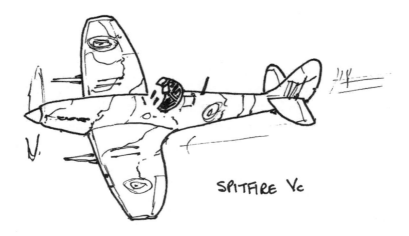

SPITFIRE Vc

The late Joy Lofthouse, an Air Transport Auxiliary pilot, who died in November 2017 at the age of 94, once said of flying her favourite aircraft, the Spitfire, 'It's the nearest thing to having wings of your own and flying.'

There are probably more books written about the Spitfire than any other British aeroplane; I've even illustrated one myself!* So I feel no need to give any long historical or technical background to this most famous of RAF fighters. The Shuttleworth Collection's Spitfire Mark Vc AR501 was built in 1941 by Westland Aircraft of Yeovil in Somerset and issued to No. 310 Squadron, which was predominately manned by pilots from Czechoslovakia, hence the Czech Air Force roundel painted on the side of the fuselage, just beneath the windscreen. AR501 later served with the RAF Gunnery School at RAF Sutton Bridge in Norfolk.

---

* *Spitfire at War* by Alfred Price, published by Ian Allan Ltd, December 1974.

After the war the airframe was used for technical instruction at Loughborough College until it was acquired by the Collection and restored to flying condition for use in the 1969 film *Battle of Britain*. Although the battle took place in 1940, when only Mk I and Mk II variants were available to the RAF, there were only two of those in flying condition at the time. Hence the producers had to use seven other marks for the aerial sequences, and AR501 was one of those. After filming the aircraft was stored at Old Warden for three years before a further and more rigorous restoration to her original condition and markings. Originally restored with conventional wingtips, clipped wings were fitted later. AR501 was fitted with a 1,585hp RR Merlin 45 V-12, water-cooled engine.

The Spitfire is a legendary and iconic aircraft that, somewhat incorrectly, most of the public thinks won the Battle of Britain. In fact, twenty-nine Hurricane squadrons and nineteen Spitfire squadrons took part. Nevertheless, this does not diminish the pulling power of the Spitfire at air displays around the world. Astonishingly there are now no fewer than thirty-one airworthy Spitfires in the UK, with another sixty-four under or awaiting restoration and sixteen on static (non-airworthy display). That is a total of no fewer than 111! Worldwide the figures are 54, 71, 113 and 238 respectively. To fly a Spitfire is every pilot's dream – if it isn't, then it should be!

The day that the Collection's chief pilot, John Lewis, came to me and said in his laconic manner, 'Brookie, I think it's time you learned to fly the Spit,' was a landmark in my flying career. I was 52 years old, by a few days, and I had more than 7,000 flying hours in my logbook, gained on well over 100 types, and mostly one hour at a time. Obviously I had hoped that this day would come when I first joined the pilot list at Old Warden – now it was here.

I already had a set of pilots' notes, purchased many years before, and they were for the Mark V. I had read them many times, dreaming quietly of the day when I might climb aboard a Spit and get air beneath its wings. However, that didn't mean I could cut any corners. The first order of the day was to get aboard AR501, with air beneath the wings, but this time on jacks in a hangar! This was so that I could practise raising and lowering the undercarriage, which is operated hydraulically. The operating handle is on the right wall of the cockpit and is mounted on a fairly large circular selector. Once the groundcrew had the hydraulic rig up to speed, I was given the signal to retract the wheels. The handle at the lower end of the selector had to be moved inboard, not far, and then moved smoothly and unhesitatingly up to the top of the selector, where it was moved outboard into a slot; it seemed to do this on its own. Sitting in the open cockpit, even with the rig hammering away, the sound of the wheels moving up and locking into place, one at a time, was clearly audible. Two indicators mark that retraction is complete: a red UP light on the instrument panel and another indicator marked 'idle' on the selector. I reckoned that after take-off it would be easy to check the first, but I wouldn't want to be peering into the bowels of the cockpit for the other. Having got the gear up successfully, it was now time to reverse the operation and lower the wheels, which locked down with a satisfying clunk! The undercarriage down light came on. The important thing was not to pause on the way up or down with the selector, as this could cause the locking mechanism to malfunction, with expensive and embarrassing, not to say dangerous, results. After a couple of more practices the real guardians of the aircraft, groundcrew such as John Stoddart and Andy Preslent, declared that I was safe to be let loose in their baby. As I climbed out I resolved to make sure that I wound the throttle friction hard on, so that when I changed hands to operate the undercarriage selector, the throttle didn't slide back, with more potentially disastrous results!

The day soon dawned when the Spitfire had my name on it (not literally!) and I walked out across the grass towards the beautiful fighter. A couple of the other Spitfire pilots had given me advice, but the words I remember best were from Dave Mackay, who is now a test pilot for Richard Branson's Virgin Galactic programme. Dave said, 'Don't worry about it, Mike, you'll enjoy it. Just think of it as a Chipmunk with a big engine – it'll go really well and make lots of noise!'

After walking round to check the condition of all the panels, the security of the fasteners around the engine, and making sure that the pitot head cover had been removed from the sensor near the starboard wingtip, I climbed onto the rear of the port wing, walked up and stepped through the open, drop-down door onto the seat. Holding the top of the windscreen arch, I let myself down into the cockpit. The trolley-acc was alongside the right side of the nose but I couldn't see it because the wing leading edge was in the way. Surprisingly, this was the first time that I really noticed how far back I was sitting. It was not unlike the DH.88 Comet, except that there were no engines on the wing to make things worse.

I adjusted the rudder pedals and then strapped in, looking around the cockpit as I did so. The cockpits of the early Spitfires were relatively simple and fairly well laid out, so I didn't expect too much hunting around to find things; and that was indeed the case. The spade grip-topped stick flopped about a bit, so I parked it out of the way, selected the brake lever on and locked it. Approaching the time to kick the Merlin into life, I turned the fuel cock on and unscrewed the Kigass primer knob, ready to give it a few shots. I gave a wind-up signal to the small collection of men outside and set the throttle about half an inch open. As this was to be the first flight of the day I hit the pre-oiler button for thirty seconds to lubricate the important moving parts inside the Merlin before start-up; this system reduces wear and tear. I heard the pump running and a light on the instrument panel came on; I made sure it went out when I released the button – and the noise stopped. Now to prime the engine with a few strokes of the Kigass pump, switch the magnetos on and press the booster coil and starter buttons on the lower part of the instrument panel. The prop turned and I was ready to use more primer if the engine didn't fire. But with a fair bit of smoke and that well-known throaty crackle the Merlin came alive. I screwed down the primer and selected the battery switch on.

The engine soon settled at a fast tick-over and, after checking yet more items, such as the radiator flap, brake pressure and the dead cut of each mag-neto, it was time to wind the engine up to 2,200rpm to check the operation of the prop and magnetos. Another wind-up signal sent two burly chaps rearwards to lie over the tail while I put the power up. By the time that was over and the engine was idling nicely again, I noticed that the coolant temperature had climbed quickly, a characteristic of early Spitfires with only a single radiator. That prompted me to get a move on. I was going to take-off on the south-easterly, slightly downhill runway, which was but a short distance from where I had started up, so I carried out the pre-take-off checks before I moved off.

The Spitfire was fitted with a VHF radio, which I had switched on before starting the engine. As this was the morning of a display day I made a call to announce that I was about to move onto the runway for departure so that the man in the tower ('Warden Radio') could ensure that any arriving air-craft were fully aware of the 'heavy metal' departing to the south-east. I held the stick fully aft, waved the chocks away and set about 1,200rpm. As we rolled forward I rechecked that the rudder trim was set to fully right, to help overcome the swing to the left on take-off. I also ensured, yet again, that the throttle friction nut was good and tight!

Taxying and manoeuvring was no problem, except for being unable to see through the Merlin. I swung around onto the runway, rolled forward a few yards to make sure that the castoring tailwheel was straight, held the stick fully back, applied the brakes and slowly moved the throttle forward until I had about 1,500rpm. *Well, Brookie, this is it – it's finally your turn to fly a Spitfire – don't mess it up – lots of folk are watching!*

I released the brakes and progressively opened the throttle, trying to match the yaw with rudder as the speed increased. I checked the boost, it was still well below the max of +12psi and the speed was going through 70mph. I allowed the stick to move forward a little and the tail came up immediately. Being aware of the limited distance between the propeller and the ground, I held the top of the nose just above the far horizon and made sure we were still going straight down the strip. At 90mph, following a small rearward tweak of the stick, we were airborne and accelerating rapidly; I squeezed and released the brake lever to stop the wheels rotating as they retracted. Now for the hand choreography – left hand to the stick, right hand to the undercarriage selector handle, pull out, lift smoothly up, push in, check the lights – all good – change hands back to normal. The power had not trickled back and I don't think I'd let the wings waggle!* After a few more seconds all the right indications were there to show that the wheels were up and locked. *Gosh! It's noisy in here. Dave Mackay was right!*

At 140mph I raised the nose from the very shallow climb I had held over the airfield, throttled back to +6 and 2,650rpm and adjusted the attitude to give a speed of 170mph. The plan for this first sortie was for me to fly to Duxford and carry out two or three landings and then stop for fuel before practising my display there a couple of times; after that returning to Old Warden and land. The reasoning was that the runway length at Old Warden was limited and could be a bit intimidating for a first-timer like me. It also gave me the opportunity to practise my display routine without being inconvenienced by the arrival of visiting aircraft. Duxford had been pre-warned and two SVAS guys had gone over in advance to help me with the turnaround.

En route I climbed to 8,000ft to further explore the Spitfire's flight envelope and handling. The climb rate of 2,500ft per minute got me there in three minutes and I throttled back to zero boost and 2,000rpm, which gave a speed of 180mph. I re-trimmed the rudder to remove the extra bias I had used on take-off, checked all the temperatures and pressures and moved the

---

* It was said that you could spot most first-time Spitfire pilots because the wings would waggle when they changed hands to get the wheels up.

radiator shutter to almost closed (there is a mark by the lever that shows the ideal position for minimum drag). There are two fuel tanks in AR501, both between the pilot and the engine; the top tank holds 48 gallons and the bottom tank 37, a total of 85. At 180mph the fuel consumption is about 45 gallons per hour; however, at full power it can be well over 120gph!

I tried some climbing and descending turns and found that all that I had heard was true. You just have to think about doing it and it happens. The longitudinal stability was not strong, so there's no need to constantly keep trimming. This is a thoroughbred – responsive and eager to please! However, I noticed that changes in speed did cause changes in directional balance. But all the controls are so well harmonised that everything is easy – you just have to have a heightened awareness to fly the aircraft as neatly as it deserves.

Before attempting more exciting stuff, I throttled back, instantly rewarded by that snap, crackle and pop of the now over-rich Merlin's exhaust backfiring a little. As the speed dropped to 100mph I made a turn to check below and then selected a heading for a straight 'clean' stall. At 80mph I could hear and feel the airflow breaking away from the canopy and at 75mph I could feel a definite buffet on the stick; the stall proper occurred just a few mph later, with a definite nose-down break and a tendency for the right wing to drop. Recovery with a nudge of forward stick was instant and as the power came on we were soon climbing again – with lots of rudder to compensate. With the undercarriage and flaps down the stall speed was about 10mph slower and equally well behaved.

I cleaned up the aircraft, applying +6 boost and 2,650rpm as I did so; this was the power setting that I expected to use for displays. I visually cleared the area and cross-checked where I was. Having trained to fly Canberras at RAF Bassingbourn, I instantly recognised a unique feature: a long, wide avenue that led to the stately home of Wimpole Hall. I was about halfway between Old Warden and Duxford. Working to a base of 2,000ft, I flew a series of wingovers, half Cubans, a barrel roll and an upward aileron roll or two. I also tried a loop from an entry speed of 300mph and she went around like a dream. The speed varied from 300mph to less than 100 over the top, where a bit of gentle handling was necessary. I watched the sideslip like a hawk and flew very gently as the speed approached the lower numbers. It was going to be possible to fly a spirited display without using any more than around 3g. With that knowledge my confidence was boosted and I started to realise why all those guys who had got into Spitfires before me didn't want to share!

Now it was time to go to where a lot of those guys flew from – Duxford. I called on their published frequency and got a crackly reply.

'Spitfire India India, you are clear to join the circuit, there is no other traffic, report downwind for runway 06 – do you want to use the grass?'

'Affirmative,' I replied. *Landing on hard runways comes later!* I thought.

I flew to a downwind position at 800ft and 120mph, lowered the undercarriage, set the rpm lever fully forward, the radiator fully open, checked the engine gauges, fuel contents, opened the hood, locked it back and checked the brake pressure. Opposite the end of the grass strip at 100mph I started a descending turn, lowered the flaps about halfway round the turn and aimed to roll out at 200ft with the speed at 80mph. As I was practising for the shorter runway at Old Warden I would try to have about 75mph over the threshold. Because of the Spitfire's immaculate handling qualities, it all worked out as planned. As I rolled out I naturally lost direct sight of the strip, but it was no worse than being in the rear cockpit of a two-seat Jaguar and I used the peripheral cues to keep straight. I held off at what I thought was about 6in and as the nose rose to the three-point attitude, which I had memorised from taxying, I stopped moving the stick, made sure that the throttle was all the way back and she settled onto the ground very gracefully on three points. It felt so good that I thought that I'd better go round and prove that it wasn't a fluke. So, using the small switch on the upper left of the instrument panel, I raised the flaps and, oh so carefully, applied power. As I didn't have the rudder trim pre-set to help this time I really noticed the need to apply lots of left rudder. I also slipped my left hand down from the throttle to wind the friction nut tighter.

The second circuit was virtually identical to the first with another very satisfactory arrival; there was enough fuel and time for just one more. The Spitfire is legendary not just for its operational record but because it is one of those aircraft that flatters anyone that flies it properly. Of all the modern aircraft I had flown I had rarely found that; the Hunter, Lightning and F-15 Eagle were three that come to mind. You start out thinking that it might be too challenging and it turns out to be far from that.

I turned off the grass runway and spotted my guys waving to indicate where I was to park. After shutting down and climbing out I realised just how noisy it had been in there! The fuel truck was already there ready to top up the tanks, so I left them to it and strolled over to the control tower to check that they knew what I was going to do next, and visit the facilities!

When I had planned my Spitfire display I chose to replicate much of the display sequence I had worked up for the Hawker Hunter T.7.[*] One thing I had decided early on, and in line with advice received from one of the best classic aircraft display pilots that I knew, Dave Southwood, was that I would not include any manoeuvres that involved me pulling earthwards through the horizontal from the inverted, such as loops or half horizontal eight positioning manoeuvres. One reason was that I knew of several professional pilots who had died at airshows doing those particular aerobatics; another was that with civilian high-performance aeroplanes there was usually not enough money to finance lots of practice. So the principle was to keep it simple, and not stupid! I also don't believe that precious warbirds should be put through a continuous aerobatics display.

My Spitfire display would be as follows: a curving low-level arrival at 350mph from crowd right, roll out on line at 200ft, at crowd left pull-up to about a 60 degrees climb, roll left through 300 degrees and pull over into a right wingover. Head back in a descent to crowd centre and make a 360 degrees turn at 60–70 degrees bank, 200ft and 300mph onto the display line. At crowd right pull up into a half Cuban, descending on a 45 degrees line into a barrel roll to the left, recovering at 45 degrees away from crowd left and then pulling up into a wingover and, at Old Warden, lining up with the other runway for a low flypast at 90 degrees to the main display line. Another high wingover used to regain the main line from crowd left and flypast at 200ft and 350mph. Now another half Cuban but descending into a full turn opposite crowd centre, roll out on line and pull up at crowd left into a double aileron 'Victory' roll. This would signify the end of the display and I would then fly to downwind for landing.

However, my first public display was to be back at Duxford on Bank Holiday Monday, 6 May 1996, where I would join a baker's dozen of other Spitfires for the Spitfire's Diamond Jubilee Airshow. For this display I was required to show that I could fly in formation safely, so an arrangement had been made with another Spitfire for me to join up for a few manoeuvres. Thankfully that went well and we landed and went to the briefing for the day's flying. There I discovered that I would not be part of the massed flypast, which was a disappointment, but would join with Jonathon Whalley's Mk I Spitfire and a Duxford-based Hurricane for the opening sequence.

---

[*] This was civilian-registered Hunter T.7 G-BOOM operated by Jet Heritage (see Chapter 18).

This was to be a 'scramble' to see off a Luftwaffe intruder, which was to be represented by Lindsey Walton in his Messerschmitt 108 *Taifun*. After the sequence was complete I would be cleared to exit stage right and return to Old Warden. Before leaving there that morning I had received agreement that I should practise my full display when I returned. There was no display at Old Warden that Monday. Shuttleworth airshows had taken place on the Saturday and Sunday, when I had displayed the DH.51, S.E.5a, Avro Tutor and Tiger Moth.

At the appointed hour the Messerschmitt arrived and started beating up the airfield, at which point the three of us started up, taxied out and took-off. We joined up in vic formation with the Hurricane leading and climbed overhead. At about 1,500ft we went into echelon and then followed each other down to pounce on poor old Lindsey. A certain amount of ad-libbing took place as we tried to take a shot in turn, while trying to avoid hitting each other. The tower gave us a one-minute warning to end the slot so I took that as my cue to break away, fly down the runway at 200ft and 350mph in a westerly direction for my return to base.

On the way back I flew a few more rolls, turns and a loop. After that fun was over I concentrated on locating the airfield. As there would be no one in the tower, I didn't call on the radio but I flew over the top to make sure that there were no aircraft moving around nearby, then flew to the south-west of the airfield, checked that all the temperatures and pressures were in limits, opened the radiator flap and set +6 boost and 2,650rpm. Now it was just a case of diving to come from stage right in a nice curve to show off the wing shape and the Merlin's distinctive sound, straighten up at 200ft and go into the display sequence that I've already described.

As I came out of the first wingover and headed back towards the display line I became peripherally aware that there were quite of lot of faces looking at me. *That's odd for a non-display day,* I thought. *Never mind, get on with the job in hand, lad!*

Ten minutes later I was turning finals, flaps down shaping up to land – last look speed 75, that's fine, power off, keep holding off – three point attitude – hold everything and down we go. A couple of bounces later I retracted the flap, applied the brakes and came to a walking pace with plenty of runway left. *Very nice – what an amazing day. I bet I don't get many more like this one before I die!*

I followed the groundcrew's signals, parked, let the engine run at 900rpm while I checked the magneto dead-cut, then pulled the slow running cut out and silence returned. My ears were still ringing but my heart was sing-ing. I unstrapped, stood up and was greeted by another noise over the crackling of the cooling exhaust – it was applause. There were hundreds of people standing by the fence; I'd obviously inadvertently given them a treat. I walked over and from chatting with some of them I discovered that they had tried to get into Duxford but had been turned away; the place was full and the traffic jams enormous! So lots of these disappointed aviation aficionados had set off to Old Warden. The last thing that they had expected was to see a Spitfire display, so when I turned up they were over the moon. I think that whatever I had done they would have been just as pleased. The nice thing was that I enjoyed it as much as, if not more, than they did!

I displayed the Spitfire only a couple more times before it broke. During a routine ground run a strange noise had come from the engine. On inves-tigation, one of the camshafts was found to be worn beyond limits so the engine had to undergo a lengthy repair. By the time AR501 came out of the hangar I had moved to the USA. But like all great events in life, this short time at the helm of one of the greatest, best-designed aircraft ever produced will stay with me for ever. Thank you R.J. Mitchell, Mutt Summers, Jeffrey Quill, Alex Henshaw and all the thousands of people who brought this design to life. And to all the folks at Shuttleworth who have kept this one going for so long. Cheers – I salute you!

Part 4

Other Display Flying

17

The Harvard Team

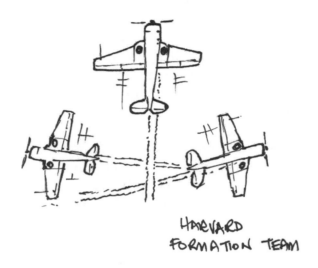

HARVARD
FORMATION TEAM

In late 1988 I was contacted by Anthony Hutton, an erstwhile racing driver and current display pilot whom I had met only once before, at RAF Finningley on the weekend when I had flown the B-17.* He said that he was looking for display pilots who had Harvard experience to join the Harvard Formation Team (HFT), which he had formed in the mid-1980s. I told him that I had flown the Harvard before and that I was likely to be flying it regularly in my new job at Boscombe Down. He invited me to go over to North Weald airfield, near Harlow in Essex, where the HFT was based, to fly with him and see whether it would be mutually beneficial for me to join the team.

Accordingly, on Friday, 11 November, I drove to Essex and met up with Anthony and Gary Numan, the pioneer of synth pop music, who owned a Harvard and was one of the existing team members. Anthony and I flew

---

* See Chapter 5.

for forty-five minutes and ran through the full gamut of the Harvard's flight envelope, except spinning. He also gave me instruction on the local area and the many complicated bits of restricted airspace due to the adjacency of London Stansted Airport. After we had landed and had a bite to eat he asked Gary to fly in the back of his aircraft, with me in the front, for a session of formation flying, with Anthony leading us. Now this I hadn't done before in the Harvard, so I hoped that I would come up to snuff! In the event, formation flying is a bit like riding a bike – once you've learned the principles it's only a case of applying them to the characteristics of the machine. In the event all went well and I was offered a place on the team. I accepted with alacrity!

As winter was approaching rapidly over the eastern horizon, no further flying with the team materialised until February 1989. However, Anthony had asked whether I knew of any other pilots who might be interested in joining the HFT. I told him that I would approach Dave Southwood, who was a tutor at ETPS, and Andy Sephton, who was also at Boscombe Down and a fellow Shuttleworth Collection pilot. They both expressed interest. I spent a few more days at North Weald in February and March, doing formation practice. On Saturday, 15 April I hired the Boscombe Down Flying Club's Jodel DR1050 and Dave Southwood and I flew over to North Weald for him to meet Anthony and Gary. That day we flew three full practices of the HFT's routine.

The team was made up of five Harvards and a Beech 18; in fact, it was a military version C-45, US registered as N5063N. The Beechcraft Model 18 (or Twin Beech, as it is also known) is a six- to eleven-seat, twin-engined, low-wing, tailwheeled light aircraft, manufactured by the Beech Aircraft Corporation of Wichita, Kansas. It was continuously produced from 1937 to November 1969; over thirty-two years, a world record at the time. More than 9,000 were built, making it one of the world's most widely used light twins. The one used in the HFT show was usually flown by the late Pete Treadaway.* It carried the markings of the RAF Far East Air Force VIP transport unit. There was a small pool of Harvards to choose from, in a variety of paint schemes. Most were in some form of Second World War camouflage with RAF markings, but one had the distinctive silver, red and yellow scheme of the US Navy. Not to be outdone, Gary's Harvard was painted to look like a Japanese fighter, with all-over white and red 'rising sun' roundels. All the

---

* Pete Treadaway was killed on 30 June 1991, when the DH.89 Dragon Rapide he was displaying at Audley End in Essex crashed.

team's aircraft were fitted with a smoke system, which pumped diesel oil into the exhaust pipe. There were different ways that these were activated, so we had to remind ourselves which aircraft we were in before that first 'Smoke! Smoke! Go!' call came! Furthermore, not all the team's mounts were flown by their owners, so we had to be especially careful drivers.

The HFT show came in two parts. The Beech 18 would lead the four RAF/USN Harvards in the arrival flypast, usually with smoke. Then there would be a turnaround and change of formation, after which the Harvards would depart the scene and leave the Beech to mooch around in front of the crowd. It was at this point that Gary would appear in his Japanese Zero looka-like and swoop down on the Beech. A bit of evasion would take place, but to no avail and Pete would activate the 18's smoke system in its port engine and disappear over the nearest horizon as if shot down. That marked the end of the Beech 18's participation. However, the Jap victory would be short-lived as the rest of us would then fall upon the enemy and take it in turns to 'have a go' at Gary. Usually one of us, whoever had drawn the short straw that day, would be shot down before the others despatched the aggressor.

Then, in a sort of time-warp peace treaty, four, or sometimes all five Harvards would join up again and carry out a variety of flypasts and manoeu-vres in formation, culminating in some type of break to land or depart. The whole thing took about twenty minutes, lots of smoke was dispensed, noise made and fun had. There were times when the Beech was not involved at all so the sequence started with all five Harvards.

During the seasons that I flew with the HFT the display developed, changed and generally got better. We flew at many venues in the UK through the summer airshow season and most shows went off without inci-dent. However, on Sunday, 23 July 1989, during a display at, of all places, Old Warden, I was flying G-CTKL, a Canadian Noorduyn Aviation Harvard IIB, built in 1941 with the original RAF serial number FE788. That day I had drawn the short straw and was due to be Gary's first Harvard victim. So when the time came I fought myself into Numan's 12 o'clock, switched the smoke on and flew off scene, over the trees and descended out of sight of the crowd. I stayed low over the fields for half a minute, switched the smoke off and then climbed to go to the rendezvous point, just south of the town of Biggleswade. There I was to lurk at 1,500ft until the team had finished the rest of the show and then join them for our return to North Weald.

As I climbed I identified the town and aimed about one mile south of it. The weather was perfect, with just a light southerly breeze. There had been

many days of great summer weather for the last few weeks. At 1,500ft I levelled off and eased the throttle back. As I did so the engine just died. The
instant thought was *What did I do?* The desire was to reverse it, and open the
throttle again, but that didn't make sense. I lowered the nose to get the gliding
speed of 80kt and looked for a decent field to land in. There was a cut wheat
field dead ahead. As I aimed for that I noticed that the prop was still wind-
milling – so the engine had not seized. I reached down to the left for the fuel
cock and turned it to 'reserve', hoping that fuel might reach the engine before
I reached the field. However, I was far too busy to peer down into the gloom
of the cockpit floor to check the fuel levels. But nothing happened. Now for
a big decision. I was nicely set up to land in the field and I reckoned I would
have enough space to stop. The decision was whether to lower the wheels or
not. Conventional wisdom in a taildragger is to leave it up, so that should the
surface be soggy or rutted the aircraft will be less likely to turn over. But following weeks of very dry weather the first was unlikely and having just been
cut I didn't expect any big ruts. So I dropped the wheels – which went down
under gravity. I really didn't want to damage this good-looking veteran that
had already been flying for three years before I was born.

As the prop was still turning I reckoned that there would probably be
enough hydraulic pressure to lower the flaps, so, as I went through about
200ft, I selected them down; and down they went. I rounded out over the
track that marked the near boundary of the field, held off until the three-
point attitude appeared around the nose and she dropped on. I held the stick
hard back, braked and we came to a stop in about 200 yards. On the way
down I had put out a 'Mayday' call on the Old Warden radio frequency, just
to let the team know that I wouldn't be joining them for the flight back.
I also knew that my wife, Linda, and her mum were at the show, so I hoped
that they could be told.

After a grateful sigh of relief and a quick prayer of thanks, I turned everything off and got out to inspect the aeroplane. As I climbed down from the
wing my flying suit leg ripped – whatever next? However, apart from lots
of straw around the wheels, there was nothing to show for the two minutes'
drama. I got back in to the cockpit and looked at the fuel gauges. Had I run
out of fuel? I remembered that when I had picked up the aircraft that morning she was not quite full, but that was not critical for the day's programme
of two twenty-five-minute transit flights and a twenty-minute display. There
had been more fuel in the left tank than the right, so I flew from North
Weald to Old Warden using that tank. When I strapped in for the display

I selected the right tank, which definitely had most fuel, despite it being hard to see what it was reading. However, I knew from my morning inspection that there were about 20 gallons in there.

When I got back in and peered hard into the gloom I could see that the right tank gauge was still reading around 20 gallons but the left tank was empty. *How on earth had that happened?* I couldn't understand how the left tank had been feeding the engine when I had selected the right tank. *Hey ho, whatever happened, let's deal with more important stuff – like how I get out of here and get home!*

As I was climbing down to go and find anyone at the farmhouse that I could see on the near horizon, the sound of four Pratt & Whitney motors floated down from above. I waved to the team; the back man waggled his wings. *Cheerio, chaps – see you sometime!* As I reached the track that led up to the farm, I saw a police car approaching. I hoped that this was going to be a useful encounter and they weren't going to arrest me for landing without the owner's permission!

In the end they were two jolly coppers who agreed to call Old Warden and let them know that I was safe and that I was at Spring Farm alongside the A1, south of Biggleswade. I asked them to pass the good news to my wife so that she could pick me up on the way home. An hour or so later I was on my way back to Boscombe Down, reunited with my lady and my mum-in-law.

Anthony and an engineer went back a few days later to see whether they could fix the aircraft and fly it out. By then I had told him that I suspected something wrong with the fuel system. On inspection they found that the fuel selector had been damaged in such a way that it didn't matter which tank I put the selector on, it was taking fuel from the left tank. They replaced the fuel selector valve and Anthony boldly took off from the field and flew G-CTKL back to base. The broken valve was mounted on a small plinth and I was given it at the annual HFT dinner – a bit like a flying Oscar!

Lots of the HFT displays were memorable for various reasons. There was the time arriving at RAF St Athan when I was the last of five to land and the flaps failed to lower. I called Andy Sephton, who was not far ahead of me, to stay on the right as I overtook him! At the 1990 North Weald Fighter Meet we incorporated a three-ship crossing break flown towards crowd centre. Before the show the three of us could be seen walking it through; always a bizarre sight! In the event, when we came around to fly directly at the crowd we wingmen dropped back to allow enough space behind the leader so that we could break towards each other and pass behind him without colliding with each other, all with smoke on. As we did that the leader (I think it was Dave Southwood) pulled up into a half Cuban. Afterwards we were told that it was quite spectacular!

But perhaps the most memorable display was a weekend we spent somewhere that would turn out, ten years later, to become my home for seventeen years: Normandy in France. We had been invited to display on two days at a 45th anniversary celebration of D–Day, to be held at the site of a wartime advanced landing ground (ALG). Following the initial invasion of 6 June 1944 a huge effort was put into building ALGs along the coastal region of Normandy, so that Allied fighters and bombers could extend their range over the ongoing combat zones by refuelling on the Continent and not having to use precious fuel crossing the English Channel on every sortie. Airfield construction teams were landed via the Mulberry Harbour at Arromanches and they built a huge number of rudimentary airstrips. This particular ALG site had been located by a local enthusiasts group, cleared by farmers and a 1,000m landing strip had been recreated. In 1944 the display venue had been ALG B7, a British landing site to the north–east of the city of Bayeux.*

It was decided that the team would fly out on Friday, 1 September to preposition at Caen Carpiquet Airport for the show on the following two days; Anthony said that we could take our partners/wives/girlfriends. Linda decided that she would very much like to join in. However, I could not leave in time to join them, so I said that I would fly out early the following day. As it happened, Gary Numan was in a similar position so it was agreed that we would fly out together. After a very early start we met up with Gary and his then girlfriend Tracy, climbed aboard our machines and set off in formation for Southend, where we would clear customs. By mid-morning we were cruising down the French coast at 3,000ft, from Le Touquet, past Dieppe, over the amazing white cliffs at Étretat and on beyond Le Havre towards Caen.

After landing we met up with the rest of the team and had coffee in the local flying club. After that the ladies departed to the display venue *en voiture*, while we briefed for the show. We were without the Beech 18 so it was just the formation part of the show plus a couple of extras but no shoot-down

---

* Normandy ALG B7 Martragny, 1,200m long, 40m wide, Sommerfeldt wire-mesh. RAF users: 19, 65, 122, 198, 609, 164, 183 and 160 Squadrons.

sequence. It was only a few minutes flying time from Caen and we went straight into the show on arrival. Landing on the semi-prepared ground had been tested by the others on the Friday – only Gary and I were going to be doing it for the first time. As someone had already pointed out after my unscheduled arrival in a wheat field in July without motive power, landing on an erstwhile maize field with the engine going should be a piece of cake! On the final break we left plenty of space between the aircraft and it was all over with no drama.

We received a great reception and were soon plied with French country hospitality. *Moules marinière* appeared in a big pot, accompanied by trays of *frites*. Beer, wine and *pastis* were also offered. As we had parked the aircraft for the night we all felt free to accept the generous hospitality – so as not to offend our hosts, you understand! Gary, not being a drinker and not liking mussels, was plied with steak, chips and coke – this made him a very happy bunny!

Even more generous hospitality was shown as we were all allocated to members of the French organising committee for overnight accommodation. Dave, his lady Deri, Linda and I were transported to a nearby village where we stayed in great comfort with a charming French couple, who plied us with many wonderful things for breakfast.

Before we went to the venue for lunch, the Sunday started with us watching a religious ceremony that dedicated a memorial to the people who made and used the ALG. The show started with a re-enactment of the construction effort. I was amazed at how they had got hold of so many functioning specialist vehicles. Then the first flying arrivals came and made flypasts; the heavier metal such as a P-51 and a P-40 did not land but some of the other, lighter slower aircraft did. Soon it was our turn, so we started up and gave a repeat of the previous day's show, returning to Caen afterwards. There we met up with our passengers again, topped up the fuel tanks and set off in formation for Blighty.

Almost two hours later we arrived at Southend and Anthony put us into echelon starboard. As we swooped down along the runway he called for smoke – so on it went. That started coughing complaints from the back seat. I knew that the smoke got into the cockpit – every time it's used there's that burning diesel smell. What I didn't realise was that it came into the rear cockpit much more; I told Linda to hang on – it wouldn't be long before I could turn it off! Silence!

After we had cleared customs, off we went again. Apparently the airport management had asked whether we could do a formation take-off and flypast for all the Sunday evening sightseers. Always keen for publicity and eager to please, Anthony had agreed. So we started up and taxied out in a rather ragged imitation of the Red Arrows and lined up across the runway. I was the back marker and there wasn't room for five abreast so I tucked in between the lead and number two and about 100 yards back. I should have known that the call before 'Rolling now' would be 'Smoke, Smoke, Go!' I let the four roll a few seconds and then set off with the aim of staying on the deck a little longer than them, gain a bit more speed and avoid the worst of the slipstream. In theory that was fine. In practice it was like an IFR take-off, with lots of smoky, squirly air all around me. However, I did get airborne safely and slid out to my position on the right. After the flypast we finally set a heading for home!

By now sunset was approaching and the light levels were getting low. There was a north-easterly wind and landing at North Weald in that direction in near darkness was not going to be easy. Anthony sent word by radio to get some vehicles to illuminate the grass strip alongside runway 02 so that we could see to land safely. Sure enough, when we arrived overhead there were half a dozen pairs of headlights doing just that. That was one landing at the end of a very long day that I was really glad to make. And we still had a long drive back to Wiltshire! But for a unique weekend like the one we had just spent it was all definitely worthwhile.

At the end of 1990 and my second season with the team I decided that I was spreading myself a bit thin across the historic display scene; I was flying with the Shuttleworth Collection and about to join Jet Heritage. It was time to say farewell to HFT. Also the drives around the M25 to Essex seemed to be taking longer and longer and I wasn't getting any younger. So I reluctantly told Anthony that I would step down – I knew there were some other candidates waiting in the wings.

I look back on my two seasons with the HFT with great fondness. The flying was both challenging and fun, but it was the people that made it; not only those in the air but also those on the ground. Anthony led the team with sanguine wisdom and, with his wife Samantha, he was always a generous and urbane host. His and Samantha's venture in starting and building up The Squadron as a very believable Second World War venue and flight support facility was admirable and brought a whole new aspect to activities at North Weald.* As far as I know they are still involved, if somewhat remotely from France, where they now live.

---

* See www.thesquadronbar.co.uk

Among other team members that I remember, apart from those already named, was Euan English, whose easy-going manner and ready acceptance of others flying his aircraft, G-TEAC, was especially memorable. In fact, he 'loaned' AC to me for two weeks in September 1990 and I was able to base it at Boscombe Down between displays at RAF Abingdon and RAF St Athan. Euan's only stipulation was that it came back safely, unbent, full of fuel and clean. As it happened there was a 1940s hangar ball held at Boscombe during that period and AC was put in the hangar, along with one of Boscombe's Harvards to add atmosphere. Syd Lawrence's Big Band played swing music and everyone dressed up accordingly. AC had been washed and polished to within an inch of its very long life! Tragically, Euan was killed flying AC on 4 March 1995 when he lost control during aerobatics. He had just bought a Spitfire as part of a syndicate; one of his lifelong dreams.

Ex-Fleet Air Arm pilot Norman Lees was another regular team member during my time with the HFT. In fact, Anthony handed leadership of the team to Norman for the 1990 season. He soon picked up the baton and led with firm precision. Norman was yet another historic aircraft pilot to be killed when the two-seat Spitfire he was flying crashed at Goodwood on 8 April 2000. I also remember Pete John and Charles Everett, but have no idea where they are now.

Gary Numan said in an interview on Quietus.com in November 2009 that he had given up the flying that he loved and sold his Harvard because of all the friends that he had lost in air accidents; many of them the people I have named. Gary was a very good pilot; there were people who would say that he was out of place doing what he did with the team. That just wasn't so. He took it seriously, had a very good pair of hands and just the right level of awareness of the dangers and how to stay safe. At the end of the 1989 season Gary gave us free tickets to his show at the Hammersmith Apollo. Anthony suggested that the men all wear dinner jackets ('black tie') and the ladies posh frocks. Having had pre-drinks at the Huttons' London flat we turned up at the Apollo and joined the queue. As we moved through the crowds, many of whom were Gary's lookalike fans, known as Numanoids, we got some very strange looks. However, the concert was great fun and it was interesting to see Gary's stage alter ego in action. He was and is a remarkable guy.

My time with the HFT was over and I wouldn't have missed it for the world. I'll finish with the team motto: 'Be there or be talked about!'

18

Jet Heritage

HAWKER HUNTER

In 1990, when I was based at Boscombe Down (for the third time!), I received a phone call from Adrian Gjertsen, whom I had met through the Historic Aircraft Association, for which I was the honorary secretary at the time. Adrian was the chief pilot of Jet Heritage (JH), which flew classic jets out of Bournemouth Airport.* He was calling to see if I could help him track down a set of North American Sabre pilot's notes. I told him that I would try. I called someone I knew on the RAF Handling Squadron at Boscombe Down, the unit that writes and publishes pilot's notes and aircrew manuals, to see if he could help. He could and I was able to send Adrian the set of Sabre notes with our compliments. When I asked him why he needed them, he told me that JH

---

* Jet Heritage had been created from the Hunter One jet collection originally established by display pilot and entrepreneur Mike Carlton in the early 1980s. Mike was killed in a Republic Seabee accident in 1986 and following auctions Ian and Douglas Craig-Wood restarted classic jet operations at Bournemouth under the new name.

was about to get an early model Sabre to operate around the airshow circuit. I offered to help further, but he very politely declined!

Some months later, Adrian called me again. This time he did offer me some flying and asked whether I could come to Bournemouth to meet the present owners of the organisation and look around; he also invited Linda. We drove down to Bournemouth and met Adrian and Ian Craig-Wood, one of the owners. During our tour of the hangar and offices I was shown all the current flyable aircraft: a two-seat Hunter, two ex-Singapore Air Force Hunting Percival/BAe Strikemasters, and a two-seat Gloster Meteor NF.11. There was also a privately owned DH Venom and a Supermarine Swift undergoing restoration to fly. I was introduced to the JH chief engineer, a delightful man called Eric Hayward.

While we were walking outside the hangar I noticed a Jet Ranger helicopter parked on the adjoining pan. Linda, who was chatting to Ian Craig-Wood, said, 'Mike flies helicopters, too.' Ian came across to me and asked if I had a civilian helicopter licence; I told him that I didn't. 'Well, it would be very useful to us if you could fly the Jet Ranger as well; I'll get Adrian to arrange for you to get your licence.'

Well, that was very positive, although at this stage nothing had been said about me flying anything else! But before it got to that stage I had a couple of burning questions of my own.

'What about flying kit? And do you keep the parachutes and ejection seats serviced and current for possible use?' I asked.

The answers were all positive and to my liking – all specialist flying kit would be provided and all aircraft safety equipment was serviced as per RAF practice. By now I'd learned that many similar operations did not follow the JH example. No matter how much I might want to fly and display their jets, this was an unacceptable practice. It was now that Adrian finally asked me if I could join the small team of pilots. The answer was obvious: 'I'd be delighted!' I said.

On Thursday, 21 March 1991 my association with JH officially got under way. I flew with Adrian in one of the two Strikemasters, G-JETP. The Strikemaster was essentially a Jet Provost Mk 4 with air conditioning and armament circuitry; I put 'JP 4' in my logbook. The check flight was obviously to Mr Gjertsen's liking, as he then sent me off solo to practice the display routine that I had worked out beforehand.

In parallel with working up the JP display, with practices and a display authorisation test at Kemble airfield, I also started my helicopter course at

Fairoaks with a delightful chap called Ken Summers. By mid-May I had started leading a pairs routine with an ex-RAF flying instructor called Dick Hadlow, who flew the other JP4. We made a fairly colourful sight as G-JETP was painted all-over midnight blue with gold lettering and G-PROV was all red with black markings. Dick and I had not had much time to put anything too ambitious together, but we were willing to try our best.

On 18 May 1991 we flew from Bournemouth to North Weald to take part in a weekend airshow. After we departed my intention had been to fly at relatively low altitudes, around 1,500ft, off the coast to Kent and then cut north with the help of London radar to get into North Weald, with which I was by now very familiar! However, as I led us along the Solent north of the Isle of Wight the cloud base came down and the visibility reduced. When I could see that the top of the chimney of the power station near Calshot was almost in cloud I decided that it was time to climb.

'Hang on, No. 2, we're going up.' I looked out to my right and saw that Dick was already very close, so I increased power and eased the nose up. The cloud was not very thick and we soon found a gap between layers at around 2,000ft. I changed radio frequency and told the folks at London radar where we thought we were and where we wanted to go. As ever they were unswervingly helpful and we arrived at North Weald in good time for the display briefing. The weather forecast was not good, with a lowering cloud base and progressive reducing visibility later in the afternoon. Our slot was timed to be as the weather deteriorated. I studied my local map carefully so that we could find our way to and from the holding point, a lake about 3 miles to the north-east of the airfield. I told Dick that we'd be doing a very flat version of our little show! As we waited to line up for our departure, the Battle of Britain Memorial Flight called in saying that the weather was below their minima, so they were cancelling their slot. I knew what was coming over the airwaves next!

'Jet Provost pair, can you go straight into your show directly from take-off?'

'Sorry, we need to go out a few miles to wind these little jets up. So just give us a couple of minutes and we'll be back!' I replied. Dick and I had walked through the routine a couple of times and I wasn't going to throw a change at him now. Sometimes display organisers put undue pressures on pilots and that can bring unwanted or even dangerous consequences. We took off as a pair and I kept the speed down as I map-read my way to the lake. Once there I turned us around, told the controller that we were on our way back and wound the speed up for our arrival at 250kt.

After the bending flypast with Dick in echelon starboard on top of the turn I pulled up and rolled right to make a wingover round back onto the display line. I had to slightly overbank as we started entering cloud at about 1,200ft. By now Dick should have dropped into line astern; a very quick glance to the right proved that he wasn't there any more. I knew he would call me if anything was going awry. I rolled out and we stayed in close line astern until I got to crowd centre (sometimes known as 'datum') and then we started a left 360 degrees turn and Dick moved back into echelon. As we got back to datum I continued the turn so that we would be able to carry out a wingover turnaround to the right and Dick dropped back into close line-astern again. After that we arranged a split by Dick doing a full 360 degrees turn while I did a shallow barrel roll and turn back onto the display line. We each lined up so that we would pass each other at datum; we were doing around 180kt by now. We each then turned away from the crowd at each end of the display line and then turned towards each other for Dick to rejoin formation in line astern. As we couldn't pull up very far, due the ever lowering cloud base, I led us left and then right, increasing speed so that we could break to land in front of the crowd.

I was pleased with how it went, especially with how Dick had hung in there – I told him so afterwards. He admitted that it had been a bit challenging! But the best was yet to come. When we were at the morning briefing for the Sunday display it was announced that our efforts in the conditions had been recognised by the award of the title 'Best Display of the Day'! In Jet Provosts – do me a favour!

Another memorable day out in the JP, the red one this time, was a display at Eglinton airfield,* near Londonderry in Northern Ireland, on Saturday, 10 May 1992. Due to work commitments I couldn't join the rest of the team, who flew up the previous day. I left Bournemouth early on the Saturday and flew at Flight Level 225 (about 22,500ft) at the optimum range speed of 160kt. It seemed to take forever, but at least I arrived with fuel to spare after one hour and fifty minutes – the longest flight I ever made in a JP!

The weather was good so Dick and I could make more use of the sky and put in more upward manoeuvres. The only thing that went wrong that day was that during the show the commentator gave out my rank and the fact that I was still serving in the RAF. Of course, I was not aware of this until I landed and climbed out of the aircraft, whereupon I was met by a

---

* Now Derry City Airport.

rather irate man who berated me for allowing such things to be said; he said that he was a member of the security services. Especially, he emphasised, when we had been specifically instructed not to make such allusions bearing in mind the sensitivities and security issues during the ongoing Troubles. I was actually nonplussed because during the pre-show preparation I had highlighted the security folks' request and had not submitted any script for myself. I don't know who had, but I was not best pleased!

I gained my Bell 206 Jet Ranger rating on 22 June 1991 and was putting it to good use by regularly commuting from my home at RAF Bracknell, to Bournemouth via Fairoaks, where I would pick up the helicopter. By August 1991 I was checked out on the Hunter and in early September I flew it to Zoersel airfield, near Antwerp in Belgium. I wasn't displaying it yet but ex-RAF Tornado pilot Brian Henwood was. He was also displaying the Meteor, so the arrangement was that I would fly the Hunter back and forth and Brian would take the Meteor and then display both. It was a memorable weekend. The jets were parked randomly, without any barriers, and I found myself fending folk off the Hunter. I told people not to pull or push bits, and even had to ask one man to come out from under the aircraft as he was smoking a cigarette! I eventually persuaded the Belgians to put some barriers around our precious jet.

Brian's displays both went very well and I took notes on what he did in the Hunter. Watching and listening to the commentator, I learned that 'airbrake' in Flemish is something like '*draagebord*'. As it was a two-day show we stayed in a hotel in Antwerp and did the whole thing again the next day. As the late afternoon sun was heading toward the horizon I got airborne in the Hunter to head back to Bournemouth. The air traffic instructions were to fly at 2,000ft and call on a specific frequency for radar clearance to climb. I took off and turned onto a westerly heading, straight at the lowering sun. In the industrial haze of Antwerp I could hardly see anything ahead. I selected the radio frequency as instructed and called for clearance to climb; I got no reply. After three attempts – by now right over the city at 2,000ft trying to keep both the speed and noise down – I gave up and reselected the Zoersel frequency. It took a while to get them to understand my problem but they eventually gave me another frequency to try. This time it worked, but by now I was over the docks and heading for the North Sea. The fact that I had flown so relatively low for so long didn't seem to have upset the nice Belgian chap on the radio and he gave me instant clearance to climb; forty minutes later I was on the ground at Bournemouth.

I continued to display the JP and fly the Hunter, for which I received my Hunter display authorisation on 1 June 1993. In the middle of that month I took G–BOOM overseas again. No. 322 Squadron of the Royal Netherlands Air Force (RNAF) was holding a 50th anniversary celebration at its base at Leeuwarden, in the northern part of the country. The brief was that I would be part of a formation of six aircraft previously operated by the squadron since its founding in 1943. As the Meteor was one of those, Mr Henwood would also be there with G–LOSM!

On the big day an Italian F-104 Starfighter and a Greek F-4 Phantom had arrived to join our two jets and a Spitfire that was due to arrive from the UK. The whole thing would be led by an F-16 Fighting Falcon, which was the current mount of 322 Squadron. Dutch royalty, in the form of Prince Bernhard, was expected to be present because he flew with the squadron in the Second World War.

By noon everything was ready except that the Spitfire had not yet arrived. I was asked by the operations folks to speak to someone in UK to find out where it was. All I could discover was that Dan Griffith, who I had met at Old Warden, was on his way in the Spit, but his ETA was unknown. As time went by it was decided that the remaining five would get airborne and hope that the Spitfire would turn up with enough fuel to join the formation. In the event it didn't and we flew around for half an hour as a pretty unique five-ship. Of course, just after we landed the Spitfire hove into view! Mr Sod's Law rules – OK?

I was asked to do a solo slot while the Spitfire was refuelled and briefed for a pairs series of flypasts with the F-16. After that I refuelled, grabbed my bag and set off back to Bournemouth. The 350-mile transits were interesting because of a specific CAA limitation on our Hunter. The instrument, navigation and radio fit, which was better than RAF standard, had not been fully certificated for instrument flying rules (IFR) flight. Because of that we were not allowed to fly in what is called the 'upper air' where IFR apply, regardless of the weather. In the UK the upper air is that above Flight Level 245 (approx. 24,500ft). The reason that the certification had not been done was because it was horrendously expensive. In my opinion, yet another case of the regulating authority making things so difficult for private owners and operators that they were likely to take shortcuts or not bother with appropriate flight instruments and navigation equipment. All that meant that I had, for the first time in my flying career, flown a longish distance in a Hunter at 24,000ft; I would previously have done a similar trip in a military

Hunter at about 40,000ft. So before I set off I looked at the pilot's notes to ascertain the optimum range speed, which turned out to be the unnervingly low speed of 270kt indicated air speed (IAS). As I should have known, that proved to be just right; I arrived at my destinations after an hour's flying with plenty of fuel.

Later that year I flew displays at RAF Valley's Open Day and RAF Finningley's Battle of Britain Day. Displaying the Hunter was a real highlight of my many years of flying, especially in G–BOOM. Its all-red colour scheme, streaming white smoke against a blue sky wasn't just patriotic – it was great to look at. I always tried to make my displays flowing and smooth. Preservation of a special aeroplane meant that after the arrival at 500kt the speeds were usually not above 360kt and I kept G levels to the minimum that safety allowed. I stuck to my rule of never pulling through from the inverted; it didn't seem to affect the integrity of the display and I always had a plan for an engine failure in my mind; thankfully I never needed to use it.

Before going to Finningley I had told Adrian that I was due to leave the RAF in early 1994 and that I was going to move to Lancashire. I told him that I could no longer commit enough time to JH and he had accepted that graciously. So, during my return flight to Bournemouth on 18 September 1993, as the sun was going down, I was sure that this was going to be my last flight in charge of a jet. In fact, that rather emotional thought turned out to be wrong. I would fly another all-red Hunter T.7 with Grace Aire when I moved to Texas in 1998 and an Alpha Jet just before I finally left the RAF (again!) in March 2004; that really was the last!

Epilogue

In this book I have restricted myself to describing those vintage and classic aircraft that I flew while involved with air displays and airshows. In fact, I was fortunate to fly other old flying machines, whose owners were brave enough to let me loose in them. One of them was a 450hp Boeing Stearman that was also owned by the Craig-Wood brothers and kept at a private strip near Frensham Pond in Hampshire. The Stearman reminded me very much of the Avro Tutor and was great fun for a Saturday morning's aerobatics!

Another 'oldie' was yet another type of DH Moth. I met a man called Terry Bucket (*not* pronounced 'bouquet'!) at Old Sarum airfield, near Salisbury. Terry had just bought a DH.94 Moth Minor and was looking for someone to help him with flying it. The Moth Minor was a low-wing monoplane designed to replace the biplane Moth series and intended to give similar performance with less power. The prototype of the DH.94 was first flown by Geoffrey de Havilland on 22 June 1937 at Hatfield Aerodrome. Nearly 100 examples had been built by the outbreak of the Second World War. With a selling price of £575, the Moth Minor was popular with flying clubs keen to acquire modern monoplanes. Nine Moth Minors were specially built with hinged coupé tops instead of the open cockpit.

Terry's aircraft (G-AFNG) was one of those coupé models and was very nice to fly. On one outing I took it to the annual DH Moth Rally at Woburn Abbey. The highlight of the day was that I was able show the original handbook, which had come with the aircraft, to the famous DH test pilot John Cunningham, who was there. In one illustration I had spotted a very youthful Mr Cunningham standing by the aeroplane with an attractive young lady. When he saw it he was very pleased and surprised, and he told me that the young lady was a typist at Hatfield. I invited him to come over and sit in the

Moth Minor; he accepted with alacrity and, despite his advanced years, made a sprightly entrance to sit in the cockpit surrounded by a cloud of nostalgia.

Other 'oldies' that came my way were Bill Bowker's Aeronca Champ (G-AWNP), in which I took my mother-in-law, Phyllis Hutchinson, flying. Incidentally, I also took her up in Euan English's Harvard; a flight that included a loop – she was in her mid-seventies at the time! I also gained quite a few flying hours in Piper Cubs, most especially Peter Middlebrook's G-OCUB, in which I helped him to learn to fly. A similar type to the Cub, with its high wing and tailwheel, was the Auster Aiglet (G-APVG) which I flew with its owner Peter Dagget. Neither of these high-wing monoplanes was difficult to fly, except for landing with any crosswind component.

As I write this, it is now more than fifty-eight years since I first flew on my own as a pilot, in a glider, and fifty-six years since I first joined the RAF. It is also fourteen years since I last sat in an aircraft where the window was in front of me and I took control! Thankfully, my memory cells, aided by logbooks and helpful mates, are still fairly serviceable so I have, over the past six years, been privileged to share my flying experiences with you, my readers. Now that the adventure is over, I have a feeling quite similar to that time in the Hunter, flying into the setting sun convinced that it was the end of an era. I was wrong then – maybe I'm wrong now – maybe I will pick up my virtual pen again and try my hand at another literary genre. But then again …!

GLOSSARY

A&AEE	Aircraft and Armament Experimental Establishment
ASI	Airspeed indicator
ATC	Air traffic control *and* Air Training Corps (*cadet organisation*)
BAe	British Aerospace
BAMC	British Aircraft Manufacturing Company
BBMF	Battle of Britain Memorial Flight
CAA	Civil Aviation Authority
cc	Cubic centimetres
CFS	Central Flying School
CG	Centre of gravity
CHT	Cylinder head temperature
COEF	Commanding Officer Experimental Flying (*at RAE Farnborough*)
CPL	Commercial pilot's licence
DH	De Havilland
DHC	De Havilland Canada
DZ	Drop zone
EE	English Electric
EFS	Experimental Flying Squadron (*at RAE Farnborough*)
ETPS	Empire Test Pilots' School
FAA	Federal Aviation Authority
FCC	Flying control committee (*for air displays*)
Flt Lt	Flight lieutenant (*RAF rank = Army captain*)
G	Force of gravity
GAPAN	Guild of Air Pilots and Navigators
Gp Capt	Group captain (*RAF rank = colonel*)

HAA	Historic Aircraft Association
HE	High explosive
HFT	Harvard Formation Team
HOSM	Holme-on-Spalding-Moor (*airfield*)
hp	Horsepower
JH	Jet Heritage
JP	Jet Provost – basic trainer
MAP	Manifold air pressure
MOD	Ministry of Defence (UK)
MODPE	Ministry of Defence Procurement Executive
NATO	North Atlantic Treaty Organisation
NEC	National Exhibition Centre
NF	Night fighter
nm	nautical miles
OC	Officer commanding
PR	Photo-reconnaissance
psi	Pounds per square inch
QFI	Qualified flying instructor
RAE	Royal Aircraft Establishment
RAF	Royal Air Force
RCAF	Royal Canadian Air Force
RFC	Royal Flying Corps
RNAS	Royal Naval Air Station
rpm	Revolutions per minute
RR	Rolls-Royce
SETP	Society of Experimental Test Pilots
SNCO	Senior non-commissioned officer
Sqn	Squadron
Sqn Ldr	Squadron leader (*RAF rank = major*)
SVAS	Shuttleworth Veteran Aeroplane Society
USAAC	United States Army Air Corps
USAF	United States Air Force
USN	United States Navy
VHF	Very high frequency
WO	Warrant officer (*RAF rank = sergeant major*)

Index of People and
Places